Safety Scissors to Spectrums

Growing up in the 70's and 80's

by

Kevin Hill

ISBN: 978-1-326-87028-7

Introduction

It is often said that everyone has a book in them. I'm not sure how true this is, but if it is true then this is my book. I was inspired to put pen to paper, or rather finger to key, when my nephew was born in 2007. I noticed that by the time he was able to sit up on his own he was being bombarded with the latest touch screen technology. Of course he had the standard rattles and cuddly toys but the very fact that he was being presented with these new age devices got me thinking.

I thought writing this book may be therapeutic for me, and hopefully something that I, and my nephew could look back at in years to come and reminisce on times gone by. I unashamedly target this book from around 1974 to around 1984, a period which was instrumental in my own introduction to all things modern. It's also a reflection of what life was like for a pre-teenage boy, from TV to games, school to play and all the other pastimes that childhood sprung on me during that period. I would have liked to have attached a pair of rose tinted glasses to this book but I realise that in essence, we all already own a pair.

This book will probably appeal and mean something more to people of a certain age. However, it would be nice to think that younger readers would be interested in a world before Facebook, Google, Playstation and mobile phones.

Our parents, generally born in the mid to late forties will no doubt of seen just as big a change in technology to our childhood, as much as we do the children of today. I'm not saying that change should stop, it can't, and I for one would not be without my mobile phone and flat screen multi channel, High

Definition TV. However, I find it difficult to see when it all changed. When was the defining moment when the past become the present? Access to Doctor Who's TARDIS or George Orwell's time machine would make it so easy to show how things have changed, but that so far is science fiction.

I emerged in to this world at the very end of the swinging 60's towards the colourful extravagance of the glam rock 1970's. Of this change I have very little recollection being just a babe in arms, although I do have vague memories of early Top of the Pops, promoting (in black and white) the likes of Slade and Rod Stewart strutting and straining their vocal chords to the extreme. What do you mean what's Top of The Pops? On that note (no pun intended) I'll move into the first chapter.

Chapter 1

Television

It's no surprise that my first chapter is about the television. It was probably the first major electronic device to make it into everyone's homes. It's one of the points of interests that everyone seems to relate to. What for example was your favourite children's TV programme, or who was your favourite Blue Peter presenter are questions that can definitely date you. For the record, some of my favourites were John Noakes, Sarah Greene and Peter Duncan.

The first memory I have of any form of television was of a brown wooden effect box which stood in the corner of the living room, or front room depending on where you live. I use the word stood as it was precariously balanced on four slightly splayed legs that did not look strong enough to carry the burden, unlike today's TV's which are sat on bespoke smoked glass units. The TV was an impressive bit of technology. It was big due to the technology that was used to display the pictures, a Cathode Ray Tube. I'm not going to give you an in depth lesson on the CRT, that after all is what Google (other internet search engines are available) is for. Suffice to say this was the heart of the TV without which it would be a useless and large ornament. One thing that made the television stand out as a machine of the future to my young eyes was that it had buttons, lots of buttons.

And dials. Don't forget the dials; they were the epitome of a future world where all things were controlled by dials. Doctor Who's TARDIS used dials, what more proof do you need that this is where the future lies?

This wonderful dial adorned brown box that sucked me into a different world was unfortunately for me, and no doubt the same in every other household in the street, generally the exclusive property of Dad. He was the one who dictated when it was turned on, when it was turned off and more importantly what Channel was to be watched. This at the time was not too difficult a choice as there were only three channels, BBC 1, BBC 2 and ITV which had regional variations. Inevitably it would be BBC 1 as adverts were not deemed to be appropriate (especially at Christmas!) and BBC2 was a little less main stream. ITV started to broadcast in the mid 50's well before my time but it was and is different to the BBC in as much as it is not owned by one company but many offering regional programmes. As it wasn't being funded by licence payer's revenue had to be collected in other ways. Taking its lead from American TV it propped itself up by getting companies and businesses to advertise on its network. For trivia fans out there the first ever advert on the ITV network was for SR toothpaste.

In this simplistic time of emerging technology, it must be noted that to operate these marvellous products it was important, in fact vital, to be stood next to them. The remote control as we know it today did not exist. It is fair to say that few items required use from a distance, unlike today where products that don't come with a remote control are deemed inadequate for the task they are designed for. However, the television was one of them. For the time being, the best way for Dad, who as you remember owned the television, to change to one of the 3 channels was to get up off his comfy chair or get one of his children to do so, which in fairness wasn't a bad thing as it was generally the only time we would be allowed anywhere near it! Just like today's TV's and radios, the station needed to be 'tuned in', a process that was much more long winded then today's automatic tuning. Back then a steady hand and a great deal of patience were required to get the optimum signal. As I mentioned before, dials were the method of choice by the manufacturers in the early seventies but later on buttons became the norm and this option gave the ability to have pre-set channels on each button. The buttons extruded from the panel face and when pulled out even further could then be tuned to the desired station. I recall the satisfying clunk as my little thumb pressed down onto the button and the TV obligingly changed station on my command. Strangely the TV had more buttons than channels, which was either a foresight on behalf of the manufacturers or to use them when the other buttons stopped work through excessive pushing.

Although colour transmission had started on BBC2 in the late 1960's, our television like many households was a black and white model, colour TV's at the time were a prohibitively expensive option. For many families, ours included, the cost of purchasing your own TV was well out of reach of the household income. Televisions, along with other household items, were bought on the 'never, never', a process which involved a part payment and then monthly instalments thereafter. Credit cards and their zero percent interest rates (if you pay in full, terms and conditions apply) were not a staple product of the wallet at the time so your shiny new gadgets were obtained from the local electrical outlet and paid back for what was probably an eternity before you owned it, which by then it would be out of date. No problem, the retailer would offer you a similar, but slightly more modern and of course slightly more expensive and tempting deal to encourage you to upgrade to the latest must have gadget. But all this was of no interest to me, all I knew is a man came round each month and Mum gave him some money in exchange of the use of the brown magic box.

Things got better later in the decade as colour TV's became affordable. Again, the choice of channels remained the same but the difference of viewing pleasure increased tenfold by the splash of colour. However, the choice of a colour TV also increased the monthly payments made by the bank of Mum. But it also introduced a new enlightenment of watching the tele. No longer did the football teams look very similar in kit or the balls much easier to work out in the snooker programmes. The 21st Century was here!

Soon, the pleasure of being able to touch the TV was once again snatched away when the next invention came into our lives. The remote control gave more power back to Dad, taking away the only option we had of laying our tiny, food splattered fingers on to the TV. Not only that, but it would soon become obvious who owned the TV again. It was not uncommon that the channel was changed whilst we were watching our favourite programme. This particular style of remote was light years away from the multi coloured and multi functioned version of today. The first I remember had two buttons. One for up and one for down, the volume was still a 'get up off your seat' control. Each button was similar to an early computer mouse and gave a pleasing, reassuring click. As each TV progressed so did the remote with ever increasing features. Today, remotes are not just used for channel changing, but can also control other devices such as Sky boxes and DVD players; they can bring up sub-titles, change colour and sound settings and so much more. Looking back, it seems the future hadn't quite arrived.

It would be remiss of me not to mention that not only were there a limited number of channels, but there was also a limited number of programmes. So much so, that during many afternoons, BBC2 would show a 'test card' along with some smooth non-descript music, or sometimes just a continuous high pitched tone, whilst BBC1 would broadcast news and very little else. A concept that now, with 24 hour, 7 days a week, wall to wall programmes seems almost alien, if not a little unbelievable. Add to this, the concept of broadcasts ending before midnight and the national anthem playing prior to a long whistling sound, children's minds of today would virtually explode with laughter. The test card which filled the screen during these gaps of any interesting programmes that were broadcast was a strange image of a young girl, dressed in a red shirt and wearing a hair band, holding a stick of chalk ready to complete the as yet unfinished game of noughts and crosses. Not too strange you may think, but playing noughts and crosses with the girl was one of the scariest looking stuffed clown toy you could ever imagine! This was an image not to be viewed near bed time, especially if parents wanted an undisturbed sleep.

During the early eighties the screens started to be filled with what could be the first steps to the modern era. Ceefax was an 'interactive' information service that was accessed via a red button on the remote control. It was very similar to the information found on the BBC's red button service today although graphically less impressive. Through this service you could look up the days, news, sport, weather and other information by selecting in the right page number, handily displayed on the first screen. This service was available throughout the day although it was used in a simpler version minus the interaction feature to fill the spaces between programs. ITV also had a similar service called TeleText which operated in a similar way to Ceefax. At the end of each day transmissions would end and a very clear BBC announcer would politely inform you that todays television had finished, turn your set off and unplug it from the wall. There was to be no more television today. Go to bed. Ok, he didn't actually say go to bed but he inferred it. The BBC world globe would rotate during a period of silence. And the finale, the national anthem would play. Then silence. There would be no more TV until the morning; the late morning to be precise.

The first breakfast television was aired on 17th January 1983. BBC kicked off the change of the morning routine that we all know today with Breakfast Time, it's relaxed and laid back presentation a sharp contrast to the staid and formal suits of the day. The presenters, Frank Bough, Selina Scott (first crush for a prepubescent teenager) and Nick Ross anchored the show with bums placed on a brightly coloured sofa with equally bright jumpers. The news was light and less formal with interesting subjects rather than strong political reports and was interspersed with features such as Russell Grants astrology predictions, Diana Moran, otherwise known as the 'Green Goddess' teaching us how to stretch and keep fit and the weather reports 'Window on the weather' with Francis Wilson. Interestingly the weather report introduced the first projected style graphics replacing the magnetic stick on boards used for many years previously. Before the age of computer graphics, the British Isles were printed on to a wall behind the presenter, the weather symbols being magnetic images of the weather to come; white cloud fine, black cloud not fine, black cloud with rain drops, you get the idea. They were placed on top of the area the predicted would have that type of weather for that day. It was always funny to see the magnetic symbols fall from their placed positions due to a failure in the magnets, London getting East Anglias bad weather quite often. Compared to todays satellite images the details were basic at best and accuracy was not a key feature.

1982 was a momentous year for broadcasting in the UK, for this was the year the fourth Channel was born. The marketing department went into overdrive to come up with a name for this new exciting TV experience, thus the fourth channel was named **Channel 4**. Not over creative but informative and correct nonetheless. The excitement of the build up to this station was immense. A month or two prior to the first transmission, the station displayed a large, multicoloured and block like number four with a music sound track playing in the background. Every so often, like a giant Jenga style Tetris block, the number would break apart and spin around, returning back to its original form a few seconds later. The excitement almost went fever pitch as the time came for the announcement that the waiting was over. The first face seen was that of Richard Whitely who hosted 'Countdown', a name and numbers quiz which is still going strong today. And then, just like the build up to Christmas or a birthday, it all went flat. The wait was on for the next new channel.

As mentioned earlier, certain programmes that you watched during your childhood gave an indication of your age. No matter who you talk to, everyone has an 'I remember that' moment when discussing old shows. As you would expect from a child under 10 in the 70's, I recall a select choice of children's programmes. For example, my range of Blue Peter presenters ranged from John Noakes and Valerie Singleton to Peter Duncan and Sarah Smith, where more recent presenters include Helen Skelton and Barney Harwood, but I'm sure there are plenty in-between or before these that relate to you. I wouldn't say that Blue Peter was a programme I, or probably many children, rushed home to watch, it just happened to be on while I was having tea (that's the meal around 5 o'clock which is not lunch, lunch is a made up word for dinner which is at noon). It was informative, educational and at some points humorous, but I think most children were interested in the slot reserved for making and baking. The immortal words 'this is one I made earlier' bounded around the playground and school classrooms without any relevance to any conversation. Notable exceptions of course were products that were actually created, cookery or home economics as it is called now for example gave the little people in the house a chance to make some almost edible cake with little resemblance to the one on screen, but then we didn't have one that we'd made earlier. I'm not sure how many people actually tried to make the now classic Thunderbirds Tracey Island, the presenter made it look too difficult to start with, and I don't ever recall Mum keeping that many washing up bottles and empty toilet rolls around the house. I also doubt that at least from a fire hazard point of view, no child was allowed to make the Christmas candle mobile, a mix of metal coat hangers, Christmas tinsel and lighted candles. What could possibly go wrong?

There were many cartoons that are legendary to people of my generation, Ivor the Engine, Pugwash, The Clangers and Bagpuss to name but a few. These were created by the genius that was Oliver Posterngate and Peter Fermin, they used basic techniques, stop frame animation with cuddly toys, but Pugwash used very simple drawings with moving arms, legs and mouth operated from behind the board.

Please allow me to give you some of my favourite shows of the time, the ones that I grew up with. I know that some of these programmes are either still going or have had a 21st century makeover (not always for the best). Some get repeats every now and then on some of the minor TV channels and are thus still in the reach of anyone looking to reminisce. However, there are a few here that will no doubt never be repeated, their existence only found on YouTube and other internet sites. So if you see some here that you recognise it will hopefully jog a few happy memories, however some you may never have heard of and I would suggest you seek them out if for nothing more than pure curiosity. I would wager that once viewed you'll probably never go to view again but that small clip will be in your memory for years to come.

Bagpuss

'Bagpuss, dear Bagpuss, Old fat furry cat-puss, wake up and look at this thing that I bring, wake up, be bright, be golden and light, Bagpuss, oh hear what I sing'.
This is an all time classic stop frame animation of a shop full of old toys that magically come to life when Emily says these magic words. It's never mentioned where Emily disappears to when after she had muttered this phrase, but it mattered not as she was not an integral part of the show, her only other appearance being a couple of sepia photographs at the end of the programme. First Bagpuss wakes up, and then the other dolls too, Madeline and Gabriel who were dolls, the mice on the mouse organ come to life as does Professor Yaffle, a carved wooden bookend shaped like a woodpecker. The objects that Emily left could be anything from a ballet shoe (just the one of course), a pile of sticks and a bottle (no surprises when they made it into a ship in the bottle) or a basket which I believe turned into the basket of a hot air balloon. One of the characters, generally Madeline, would tell a story related to the object and, accompanied by Gabriel on his banjo sing a song relating to the story. The mice would then busily repair the object whilst singing in high pitched voices (they were mice after all). The newly mended item would be put in the window just in case it's careless owner happened to pass by this old shop and call in to collect it. Now I've seen plenty of lost shoes on the side of roads and pavements but not once did I consider taking them to a shop full of stuffed toys hoping that one day the unfortunate single shoed owner would retrieve it. But

11

maybe that's just me. This was a strange shop as it never sold anything so how it maintained its existence is a mystery. That being said, the overheads must have been quite low as apart from these magic dolls, no one else was employed. By the end of the programme when the story had been told Bagpuss was shattered. Cue the end sequence and verse.

'Baguss gave a big yawn and settled down to sleep, and of course when Bagpuss falls asleep all his friends go to sleep too. The mice once more were ornaments on the mouse organ, Gabriel and Madaline were just dolls and Professor Yaffle was a carved wooden bookend in the shape of a woodpecker. Even Bagpuss himself once he was asleep was just an old, saggy cloth cat, baggy and a bit loose at the seams, but Emily loved him'.

Fingerbobs

"Yoffy lifts a finger, and a mouse is there, puts his hands together, and a seagull takes the air, Yoffy lifts a finger, and scampi dart about, Yoffy bends another, and a tortoise head peeps out. These hands were made for making, and making they must do."

The show was presented by the above mentioned Yoffy, a bearded hippie with receding long grey hair who made finger puppets from paper and card to resemble a selection of animals. Yoffi would wear a soft cloth glove of differing colours depending on the creature he wished to create, the main character being a mouse attached to the end of Yoffi's index finger. Fingermouse was made using a conical shaped card, thin strips of paper for the whiskers and oval shaped card for the ears finished off with a blackened tip for the nose and circular dots for eyes. The main remit of the programme involved Fingermouse collecting various items (such as pebbles or feathers) to make up another object at the end. As of many other kids' programmes at the time each of the main characters had their own signature tune that played as they entered the screen, 'Fingermouse, Fingermouse, I am a sort of wonder mouse' was our hero's theme. Gulliver, a seagull was made from a white ping-pong ball (head) placed over a thumb and white gloves forming the body with outstretched fingers as the wings, Scampi and a tortoise called Flash (obviously) completed the main line up.

Multi Coloured Swap Shop

It's fair to say that this was the daddy of early Saturday morning TV. Noel Edmonds, Keith Chegwin, John Craven and Maggie Philbin hosted this BBC show live to the nation, a new concept at the time and fraught with perils, especially as the audience were encouraged to phone in with their swaps and questions for the famous guests. Questions also came on postcards delivered to the presenters via a plastic globe lowered from above. In a time before e-bay the only way of buying or swapping your old clutter was to either put it into the local newspaper or the newsagents shop window or sometimes in the playground where deals could be struck, but Swap Shop changed all that. Kids would ring in and offer their old board game or doll in exchange for a more expensive toy, obviously. Details would be written on a card and placed on a board which every so often was referred to, details being read out as the show toddled along. The show was not only based in the studio but had an outside broadcast where the over excitable Keith Chegwin visited different towns and cities, bounced around and swapped kids toys whether they wanted it or not. As I remember some people did well, a set of wooden dominoes for an Action man, but others did not, the kid who swapped the Action man for example. The show also included music from a current pop group promoting their latest record, visits and interviews of celebrities, a selection of cartoons interspersed the main items and there were also competitions. John Craven also presented a news section for kids built on the back of his popular Newsround programme. If you're of a certain age like me you may remember the telephone number that was not only read out time and time again during the show, but was also displayed on the front of the desk that Noel would present the show from. Remember it? 01 811 8055 ring any bells (pun most definitely intended)? The show was never as anarchic as its ITV equivalent Tiswas but it did suffer much from the dangers of live TV. When Margaret Thatcher, the then Prime Minister, appeared on the show taking calls from the viewers she got one caller who was not a child but a man who wanted to get a few things off his chest about the state of the nation, or more over his thoughts of the Prime Minister herself using colourful language to convey his message. I'm not sure the plug could have been pulled any quicker and it left an awkward situation in the studio.

For me, it was the programme to have on after getting up mid Saturday morning, having my Golden Nuggets while sitting in my pyjamas and rubbing the sleep from my eyes just before the kids next door knocked for a game of footy. Happy days.

Ivor the Engine
Another of Oliver Postgate's and Peter Firmin's creations based around the adventures of steam engine driver Jones the Steam and his faithful steed Ivor the Engine. The stories are set in an idyllic corner of north Wales on the The Merioneth and Llantisilly Railway Traction Company Limited railway line. The requirement to give each character a title in their name relating to their occupation seems to be more than giving them a genuine surname. Apart from the main character of Ivor we had Evans the Song the choirmaster of the Grumbly and District Choral Society, Dai Station the station master and Owen the signal who as you would expect controls the signals. There were other characters that pop in and out, Idris the dragon who lives in an old extinct volcano conveniently situated just outside the town

14

and bizarrely an elephant keeper from India who keeps an elephant from the local circus. All the things you would expect to see on your next holiday in North Wales. Story lines were thin at best, Ivor using his furnace to keep the dragon warm and the elephant helping Ivor out in the snow but the most memorable part of the programme was the noise Ivor made when chugging along. Pssst-ti cuff, pssst-ti cuff is the best way of putting it on paper. Ask anyone over 40 what noise Ivor made and you should get a response similar to this. As I said, it's not the most thrilling of kids programmes, and I wouldn't expect it to hold today's children's attention for more than a minute but for me it's one of the most endearing and one that takes me back to that time. I'd love to see it repeated on some of the main TV channels or especially some of the countless kid's channels, but alas I fear this is more than wishful thinking on my part. But I would suggest, like many of the other programmes in this listing, that when you're flipping through YouTube for crazy video's of animal antics give a quick search for one of these gems and see what you think. I guess the nearest the children of today would recognise as similar to Ivor, although the books were much earlier in the century, would be Thomas the Tank Engine.

Trumpton/Camberwick Green/Chigley

No list of classic children's TV from yesteryear would be complete without Trumpton. Like many of the other programmes it had its own theme tune and a line that anyone of my age would remember. 'Pugh, Pugh, Barney McGrew, Cuthbert, Dibble and Grubb'. These were Captain Flack's diligent group of firemen who would appear from the station to the roll call, mount the fire engine and race to the emergency. To Captain Flack's dismay there was never any fire to put out, mainly cats stuck up trees and the like. Trumpton was inhabited by the usual stereotypical people; a mayor, a florist, a milliner, a clock maker and my favourite Chippy Minton the carpenter. At the end of each episode the

15

firemen gathered together on the bandstand and played their instruments while the townsfolk danced around.

Trumpton was a follow on from the successful Camberwick Green, which was set in a different although very similar village. The opening scene is of a rotating music box, its top slowly opening and the character that appears is who that episodes story will based around. As it opens the narrator says 'Here is a box, a musical box wound up and ready to play. But this box has a secret inside, can you guess what is in it today?' Much like Trumpton there are many usual suspects, a baker, a doctor who makes house visits, a village gossip and a policeman; PC McGarry who's number is 452. But to me the most memorable character is Windy Miller who obviously is a flour miller. I mentioned before that there are some sounds that are etched in to our minds that we instantly recognise, well the sound of the windmill going around is one of them. He had the knack born from many years of flour making of being able to time his entrance and exit of the windmill and avoid getting taken out by the sails. Finally, to round off the cast is the cadets at Pippin Fort, led by Captain Snort.

In the last of the trilogy for want of a better way of putting it was Chigley. Chigley was even more sedate than the others if that was at all possible. There was a biscuit factory owned by Mr Cresswell where it seemed everyone worked until the 6 o'clock whistle when they would gather at Winkstead Hall for a dance. The Hall belonged to Lord Balborough who, along with his butler Brackett ran a small railway that seemed to run all around Chigley, Trumpton and Camberwick Green. At the end of the working day in the biscuit factory the whistle would blow and the workers were invited, or more than likely instructed to meet at Winkstead Hall where Lord Balborough would plays his organ and the workers would dance. It appears that every day was dance day in the county of Trumptonshire.

These three stop motion animated programmes encompassed all that was good about childrens TV in the 70's. They were calm and ran at a very leisurely pace, they contained no violence, story lines were of innocent occurrences and the characters, whilst slightly stereotypical were a good example of what an idyllic world we would all like to live in.

Hong Kong Phooey

'Number one super guy, faster than the human eye' I'm not sure how hygienic it is to have a dog in a police station working as a janitor but this must be standard fare in America. This must have been a very small station as there was distinct lack of police officers. The station was run by Sergeant Flint, and the only other member of staff featured was Rosemary the telephone operator. Exactly who she would send to any emergency was never made clear; fortunately for them they had a secret super hero walking amongst them. Is it Sergeant Flint? No? Is it Rosemary, the telephone operator? No? Is it Penry (short for Penrod, don't ask, it is America after all) the mild-mannered janitor? Could be!

This plucky hero to be would overhear any emergency and with a swift jump into the bottom drawer of a filing cabinet would jump out the top drawer as the one and only Hong Kong Phooey. Although he didn't actually jump out, the drawer always got stuck. Fortunately for this mild-mannered janitor, Spot his stripy cat sidekick banged the side of the cabinet releasing the masked hero. He would then proceed to jump into a cupboard hitting an ironing board and sliding into the rubbish skip outside the station, triumphantly driving out in the Phooey mobile which with a bang of a gong transforms into a ship, or boat or any other vehicle useful to solving the crime. In typical cartoon fashion bedlam ensues whilst Phooey tries to capture the villain using his 'Hong Kong book of Kung Fu' and generally making a mess of things. Meanwhile Spot is doing his best to correct the hapless hero and finally pressing button/pulling lever/banging object etc. resulting in the villain being captured. Of course our hero knows nothing of Spot's intervention and takes the credit much to Spot's dismay.

There seemed to be an influx of karate based entertainment during the seventies. Bruce Lee was flying high in the movies, Kung-Fu was a major hit on the tele with 'ah Grasshopper' and Hiiyyaa' bouncing around the playground and even the music charts were targeted by Carl Lewis's song 'Everyone's gone Kung-Fu fighting'.

Mr Benn
Mr Benn is a stereotypical Englishman wearing a black suit and bowler hat who lives in a normal terraced house in a generic street, who feels each day the need to go shopping. Fortunately for him the only shop in the street appears to be a fancy dress shop. As he enters the store there seems to be no staff to tender to his needs, but then, as if by magic, the shop keeper appeared. After the briefest of conversations, the shopkeeper suggests a particular outfit and Mr Benn duly enters the changing room to try it on. Then for some reason he decides to leave the changing room via a different door, possibly to avoid payment and he appears into a land or time relating to the type of clothing he has donned. A cowboy suit leads him to the Wild West and a knight costume sends him to medieval times where he helps a dragon. Each episode has some sort of moral undertone but doesn't overplay it. At the end of the adventure the shopkeeper appears and leads him to a cave, or a room, or a door that takes him back to the changing room where he proceeds to change back to his civilian clothes. He thanks the shopkeeper and walks back home with the object given to him during the adventure as a memento, quite happy that it will remind him of his adventure.

This is one of my favourite programmes of all time and it's a shame that only 13 episodes were ever made, but then would it spoil the magic if there was too many, who knows? Maybe only 13 were made as the shopkeeper went out of business as Mr Benn never bought any outfits, after all 13 is supposedly an unlucky number.

Captain Caveman

Captain Caveman or "Cavey" for short is a caveman who is as you would expect thousands of years old. He was discovered, not quite sure how, by three teenage girls, the Teen Angels, frozen in ice who promptly defrosted him. The Teen Angels are a crack force in solving crime (much like Scooby-Doo), and use Cavey's super powers to help them along the way. As no-one knows for sure what a caveman could do, artistic licence was given free rein to give him amazing and useful special powers. Unfortunately, standard use of the English language was not one of them. He often muttered the words Unga Bunga under his breath and spoke in typically expected caveman speech missing words like 'and' or 'the' in sentences. Did I mention he could fly? But in typical cartoon fashion it failed him at key points with obvious results. No self-respected caveman would be without a club and neither was the Captain but of course his had a little more to it than clubbing dinosaurs. When he needed to use it the end opened up and revealed a candle with enough power to light a whole room. His hairy body hides all manner of objects that he pulls out when the occasion needs and has a tendency to eat as many things as he can especially clues that would help in the investigations. The Teen Angels, Dee-Dee, Brenda and Taffy excitedly bundle around and like proper sleuths deducting that the culprit is the one man that everyone else knows did it but they have to go round the houses to find out. When an idea finally comes to light to help solve the crime Taffy cries 'Zowie!' and all is revealed.

I fondly remember the show for some of the clever tricks that Cavey brings out his fur, much like inspector gadget, and the immortal shout heard across the playground 'CAPTAIN CAAAAVVEEE MAAANNN!'. I think you'd have to be there.

Roobarb

Everyone calls this Roobarb and Custard, although its correct title is just Roobarb. Custard was Roobarbs neighbour, a pink cat. Roobarb was of course green. He had a habit of inventing things to solve problems that probably didn't need solving resulting in some sort of mishap. Meanwhile Custard would look on being generally sarcastic and making fun of Roobarbs ideas, often falling backwards off the fence. The other main characters are the birds who sat in safety on tree branches sniggering as Roobarb and Custard failed at their respective adventures. The animation was one of the things that set this apart from other cartoons, especially those slick animations from America like Tom and Jerry. The characters were drawn on a white background using marker pens and a basic animation technique which led to a sort of flickering of the characters given it a style all of its own. It was voiced by the unmistakable Richard Briers, and drawn by Bob Godfrey who also drew Henry's Cat and Noah and Nellie. Much like Bagpuss, this cartoon has become a cult classic; and rightly so.

Jamie and the Magic Torch

Who wouldn't want a magic torch? Well, Jamie was a lucky kid who had such a device and when he pointed it at his bedroom floor it would open a hole to a strange world. Jamie and his faithful dog Wordsworth would jump into the hole and whizz down a helter-skelter to Cuckoo Land. Of course a land called Cuckoo would as you expect be home to a number of strange characters.

Mr Boo who wore roller-skates flew around in a 'submachine' whatever that is, Officer Gotcha (nice name) had a unicycle instead of legs and ate truncheons, Strumpers Plunkett was orange and could play tunes from his flute like nose and of course Wellybob the cat who did everything backward. Others also popped in and out, Bully Bundy, Jo-Jo and Nutmeg and joined in the fun. A little psychedelic in colour and strange plot lines this is certainly one for its time and unsurprisingly has not been remade. The last scenes were Jamie jumping back to his bed just in time for his mum to tuck him in, 'settle down now Jamie, come on Wordsworth, out of there'.

These are some of my favourite and memorable programmes, the ones that remind me how innocent kids TV was back then. I have missed some glaringly obvious programmes out like Blue Peter, Grange Hill, Top of the Pops, Play School and Play Away and there are many, many more that I could wax lyrical about. But there are plenty of books on the market that cover all of the ones I've missed and it's worth hunting some of these down if you want to go glassy eyed through nostalgia street, which is always a nice place to go.

Today's mobile phones and tablets give access to all day TV, a concept that would seem incredible in the 70's. In a decade of space exploration and science fiction films rolling out of the cinemas, the very idea that one day we would be able to watch TV at anytime, anywhere, would have been all my dreams come true. Star Trek had portable communicators the size of a cigarette box, Battlestar Galactia had small portable TV screens and as for Star Wars, they had robots! However, for us it was just that, science fiction. It was never going to happen, that's why it's called fiction. For the time being the technology we had was still exciting and up to the minute, we held in our hands what we considered to be the future, what could possibly improve on this?

Well, for one thing, the ability to record a programme and watch it later. Sure we could watch repeats of programmes that the TV broadcasters wanted us to see to fill in their empty timeslots, and there were plenty of those, and they had the technology to do so. They had the large original reels from yesteryear that they could use as and when they wanted, generally when there was nothing else to show. Saturday morning TV was awash with black and white programmes like Black Beauty or westerns from America like the Lone Ranger. But as entertainment starved viewers we wanted more. It is taken for granted that today we can pause, rewind and record multi channels at the same time. It was not always like this. Enter the video recorder. An incredible piece of electronic gadgetry that gave us just what we needed, the ability to record TV shows at the push of a button. Actually it wasn't quite as simple as that to start with but the statement still stands. Initially there were two rival designs, BETAMAX and VHS, although there was a third, Video 2000, but this was higher end professional and never took off. It's difficult to put an analogy to this, but if I must, and I feel like I do, then think about PC's and Apple Macs, both do the same thing but are completely incompatible with each other. But unlike the computer scenario where they can quite happily co-exist, with the video recorder there had to be a winner. And, as in so many competitive genres, the winner is not always the better system, but the better marketed. It is generally agreed that although BETAMAX was the better of the two in quality, VHS won the popularity contest.

Today's Sky boxes and Freview boxes have built in hard drives allowing more programme to be recorded at once, but how did we do it in the past? Well quite simply we couldn't, but as you remember there weren't that many stations and programmes that you could watch and record at the same time. Each tape could record up to 4 hours, which was ample for most use. However great the system was, there was a downside compared to today's technology. The disadvantage of recording on tape compared to the modern hard drive recorders is that it is very difficult to zoom forward to the part you want to watch. There was a 'fast forward' and 'fast rewind' feature which worked to a degree, but you had no idea whereabouts you were in the recording. I recall having a number of cassettes, each with a list of programmes on, and to find the point I needed I would have to write the counter number for each start and finish of the shows. All well and good as long as when you first started the tape you remembered to reset the counter, and of course you didn't change the cassette in-between. But of course this was still the latest technology that crept into the living room as a shiny new statement of being the modern family. It was also another item for Mum to dust.

The TV had become the hub of the family life. Weekend evenings, specifically winter ones when we were not allowed out too late as the evenings drew in, were spent watching family programmes like The Generation Game, 3-2-1 (try explaining how that worked) and the comedy duo's of the two Ronnie's and Morecambe and Wise. We would gather round in the glow of this magical box, Mum watching the TV, Dad reading the paper and us, we were either watching the programmes or possibly reading our comics. Although the TV had become the hub it was still yet to completely dominate our lives as it does today. So, going back to the premise of this book, I have seen in terms of technology a rapid development in how items have changed over what is considered a short time. However, that short time to me has been a steady drag with the pace of change appearing to keep with expectation. I now own a large flat screen, multi-channel hi-definition TV and could find it difficult to go back to the old design and features, although in a small way I would quite happily set a room aside to put an old TV and video recorder for nothing other than nostalgia.

In the ten years or so of my early childhood I saw the huge development in the television, from an imitation wooden box with limited viewing capability, to an everyday product that the family life started to revolve around. The world of entertainment was changing. Fast.

Chapter 2

Music

As the television offered a limited amount of visual entertainment, it was the radio, or wireless as our parents often called it, that would fill the gap.

Before the advent of breakfast TV the kitchen was the place where everything happened in the morning. There was no need to be in the living room as the only form of entertainment was in the kitchen. The radio in our home was generally ensconced on the kitchen worktop, not to be moved. The telescopic aerial being the only way to ensure the channel stayed tuned in to the right frequency, pointing it in different directions to achieve the best signal, which could change daily due to 'atmospheric interference'. These were the days long before digital radio came into being, so the signal was broadcast via Medium Wave (MW) or Frequency Modulation (FM), the latter being the more reliable and better signal. And, as if more proof that the future had arrived was needed, the channels were tuned via a dial. Today we are used to the radio auto-tuning itself and finding the best station available storing them in preset channels, the details being displayed on an LCD display. Even the song, DJ and programme playing are given freely. But back then our radios had a dial which moved a plastic arm across a board marked with the radio frequency. You had to remember what frequency your station would be on, 88.9FM, 909MW and so on. To help you with this memory game each station would brashly promote their channel as much as was humanly possible, 'You're listening to local radio on 88.9 FM'. Bearing in mind that the precision of the dial and marked reference numbers were far from accurate and the slightest touch could knock you out of tune. The signal strength also played a part as the weaker the signal the more difficult it was to find; this was more prevalent on Medium Wave where interference from different countries could sometimes be heard. For example, some national stations had strong transmitters and could be picked up quite easily, even on small portable radios, the same for local stations. Others however were just out of reach and required careful positioning of the radio and fine tuning of the dial to stand any chance of receiving a signal. That hasn't really changed that much for analogue radio although radio's themselves have better aerials and can tune to the station more accurately.

Again, much like the television the choice of stations was limited. BBC dominated the airwaves with stations 1 to 4 and many local stations covering the area you lived in. Independent radio stations had yet to become main-stream so it was the Auntie Beeb or nothing. It is hard, even for me to believe that there was a time before breakfast television, but this is what it was like. The kitchen was the hub of our household, and no doubt many others, during the morning school run ritual, and in the absence of breakfast television, the radio played its part in this daily event. Along with the sound of snap, crackle and pop would be heard the dulcet tones of the radio presenter trying his best to sound enthusiastic whilst reporting on the mundane local events. Jumble sales and lost pets were the general order of the day along with some roving reporter on the streets asking questions about local issues. Again, my recollection of the radio is of a brown wooden effect box (do you see a pattern emerging), about the size of half a dozen or more Christmas annuals stuck together. A single speaker hidden behind some strategically lined slats released the slightly muffled sound. Bass and treble settings were sometimes available on certain models, but no-one really knew how to use them so they were generally left at zero. Soon we left for our daily dose of education, safe in the knowledge that on our return the radio would be silent and the goggle box would once again rule the household.

However, unlike the television, radio was not confined to the house; there was another option, a portable option in the shape of the transistor radio. Transistors were invented during the late 1940's but gained popular usage during the 1970's onwards. They were in essence the precursor to the microchip found in almost every device today. These almost pocket size music systems did work on battery power and due to the fact it had small speaker and basic features it used only a small amount of power and lasted quite a while. Roughly around the size of a modern mobile phone, but much chunkier, these pocket wonders gave us the freedom to roam around whilst listening to the top twenty charts. The antennae as such was internal to the device, which was great as it avoided the risk of poking someone's eye out with the telescopic version found on the household radio. The downside to this was the reception was poor so you found yourself twisting the radio at acute angles to receive the best signal. There was a round dial (what do I keep telling you) that was used to tune to a station, but it was very, very sensitive. One tiny movement of the dial from its location would result in losing the station signal. It was common place to find yourself listening to Radio One with a whistling or some foreign radio station in the background. Although there was a small speaker at the front the sound quality was poor and quite annoyingly tinny. They did however come with an earpiece, no need for two as it was only a mono output. These earpieces were 'designed' to fit into the ear much like the modern versions of today. They were made of some sort of Bakelite plastic, and unlike today's that sit comfortably inside your ear, these were so large that there was no way they would stay in unless you tilted your head to an almost laying down angle. The sound itself was, if possible, worse than the internal speaker so it was generally discarded in favour of sharing the music experience with friends. I fondly recall sitting outside my front door, adorned in flared trousers and stripy jumper listening to Abba singing Waterloo on my small black transistor radio. You probably have some of these moments when you hear something or smell something and your mind is instantly taken back to a particular time in your past, well every time I hear Waterloo, even after 40 years, I'm transported back to that time and place.

The seventies and eighties were filled with the sound of the latest songs from the era, plus a large splattering of music from previous decades, but all of these came via the radio. Record players were nothing new; they'd been around since the early part of the century growing popular from the sixties onwards. As the cost of these items came down they became another electronic part of the living room furniture (sorry Mum). They were not the smallest of items to fit on to a shelf as they required enough space for a twelve inch (30cm in today's money) shiny black disc to sit in the centre, along with all the buttons, sliders and dials.

I find it difficult to put into words how special it felt to open up a record from its sleeve, and then from its second protective layer to see the finely etched cylindrical lines that held the music just waiting to be released. There was also a smell, a smell again unique to its origins and what I can only describe as a newly opened book with a hint of static electricity. Ok, not the best description but the only one I can conjure up. Carefully placing the record on to the rubberised deck and slotting neatly through the spindle in the centre, the excitement and anticipation is something you could not get from any of today's technology. And then there was the crackle as the stylus, or needle as it was commonly known, gently bounced on the small particles of dust, and tiny bumps on the track made during recording. I'm not going to get into the argument of sound quality compared to today's modern MP3 recordings, this is a matter of pure personal preference, however I do think the vinyl does seem to give a lighter, natural sound, but as I say I'm no expert. The tightly packed lines gave way to small gaps indicating where one song finished and another one started giving you the option to drop the stylus into the space and jump straight to which ever track you desired. A lot of songs during this period and earlier 'faded out' towards the end of the song as if someone was walking away with your music centre and the sound getting fainter and fainter until you could no longer hear it. And then, after half a dozen songs it was time to turn the disc over to play the B side. To me that doesn't sound wrong, the term 'A' side and 'B' side mean something. On a single record, or seven inch to be more accurate, the 'A' side was where the song that was released and put into the charts lay, the flip side was usually a studio track that was never destined to hit the charts and would generally remain an album track. Occasionally artists would release a double 'A' side single, one which had two tracks that were both deemed good enough to be scattered across the airwaves. Vinyl records are now starting to have resurgence; many of the latest releases coming out on the shiny black discs and record shop are slowly starting to pop up on the high street. Long may it continue.

I recall in the late 70's my elder brother received for Christmas an Amstrad music system, which combined the radio, record player and cassette player. A nice touch of design was that the turntable was hidden underneath the unit, only to emerge sliding gently forward and backward at the touch of a button. The front was adorned with buttons and small flashing LED lights, but no dials. Dials had been replaced by sliding controls. Sliding controls were the new future. There were plenty of other makes and models all with their own unique features, but one thing they all had in common was the ability to record, or 'tape' music from the radio or record player. For the first time we had the ability to 'copy' our beloved vinyl discs to a small portable cassette tape. Tapes came in different lengths, C60, C90 and C120, the numbers corresponding to minutes in total, so for example a C90 had 45 minutes each side. The popularity of these tape formats even lent itself to a 'hit' record by Bow Wow Wow entitled 'C30, C60, C90 Go'. Don't bother looking it up, it's seriously not worth it. There were smaller sizes, C15 and C30, but these were too small to be practical for music and were used at later time for computer software, more of that later. TDK and BASF were the popular brands and considered the better quality with their 'Chromium Dioxide' technology, whatever that was. It was common to receive packs of these in your Christmas stockings along with bags of nuts, tangerines (don't ask) and the obligatory plasticine and felt tip pens. Albums were now released on cassette as well as vinyl giving the opportunity to own an official version with the album cover, track list and sometimes the lyrics that you could carry around with you.

These cassette recorders also allowed the ability to record from the radio which was used well on a Sunday evening when the top forty was aired on Radio 1. Back then, record sales were counted during the week and the results were not released until Sunday evening, whereas today the number one slot changes by the hour as songs are downloaded from music websites. No-one, well no-one outside the radio station, knew which artist would be at the top of the charts by the end of the week. It became a skill to press start and stop at the right time to avoid the DJ talking over the start and end of the record and was also the easiest and cheapest way of getting to hear the new number 1 and be able to play it back again and again to ensure that you knew the words for the playground the next day. Today you just download it from i-Tunes or similar music download websites and stash it away into the digital ether. Radio alarm clocks also started to feature cassette players giving more opportunity to listen to pre-recorded music, and even wake up to it.

Cassette players became a standard feature of all the latest music systems, many having two for tape to tape recording, which almost seems an idea that worked against the copyright of the record company and original artist. But it did provide the young computer gamer to 'copy' their games to another tape to freely swap with their friends without any regard for the legality of the process.

So now we have it, music on the move, in the house and bedrooms across the land. However, the portability of the cassette player was still elusive, that is until the Sony Walkman hit the streets. Around 1979 a brightly coloured unit, not that much bigger than the cassette itself was released and changed the way music was played. I recall a music video of a similarly brightly dressed Cliff Richard wobbling around on a pair of roller skates with a Walkman strapped to his waist and headphones straddling his head, singing a catchy little number telling the world that he was 'wired for sound'.

For a while the Walkman was the epitome of fashion and status. A product out of price for most children, but for those children who could afford it, or more like their parents could, their status and popularity in the playground was unsurpassed until the teacher confiscated it until the end of the day. Eventually cheaper brands became available, albeit of poorer build. Although cheaper in quality they still did what they said on the tin, they provided music on the go. Unfortunately, their production quality, or should I say lack of created another problem, the magnetic tape that stored all your music could sometimes get stuck around the rubber rollers inside the player. If you were lucky you would be able to catch it in time and attempt to retrieve the tape from the cassette. If you did and the reel was not too damaged, you would need to find the one tool that would complete the rescue; a pencil. To rewind the tape back in to its cassette the pencil needed to be inserted into the hole on the cassette and carefully wind back until all the tape was back in place. It wasn't always a complete cure, quite often the tape had been mangled up so much that playing it was pointless. So now you have it, the ability to record your music from your record collection or the radio, or buy pre-recorded and cassettes and listen to them outside, inside or basically wherever you want. Today we have the i-Pod or MP3 player capable of storing thousands of tracks on a device the size of a packet of chewing gum. The sound doesn't distort no matter how much you jump around and the battery lasts for days. I would have laughed you to the moon and back if you told me that in 1982!

Chapter 3

Computers

Now this is a big subject, the big subject you could say, an area of technology which has seen the most rapid and noticeable changes in the last 30 years. However, this book is about an earlier time, the seventies and eighties where things were somewhat different. We're all now used to having a computer at home, in fact those people without one are looked upon with curious, if not incredulous eyes. How is it possible for anyone to live without having any access to the World Wide Web? Computers have become as much a part of everyone's day to day life as the TV, and in many cases more. These devices which appear to make the clock go so much faster have sneaked their way into our everyday lives without us even noticing. It is so easy to get absorbed by the internet and all its many facets that those hours will zip by within a blink of an eye. That ironing will just have to wait until tomorrow.

Computers were not always like this. Modern PC's have improved exponentially in speed and power to a point now where there isn't a vast improvement on each new model. However, things were quite different in the 1970's, computers were the sole use of business, crunching numbers and data with the aim of making companies run quicker, smoother and more efficiently. They started as the size of a small room and slowly moved down to the size of a sideboard, then a fridge freezer and then during the seventies became units that would sit on the desk. These PC's (Personal Computers) were still used for business and were in effect large screen word processors and calculators. Actually that's a little unfair as they did have the ability to save and store data, produce spreadsheets and with a dot matrix printer were capable of producing effective reports. Dot matrix printer I hear you say, what's that? Before the advent of inkjet and laser printing where ink is literally jet sprayed accurately onto the paper, dot matrix printers were the norm and the only economic way of printing and worked in a similar way to ribbon typewriters. Indeed, they had a ribbon but instead of fixed hard letter hammers they had tiny metal rods, or pins, which gave them the ability to print varied font styles. Additionally, as each of these pins worked independently it was possible to print graphics and images.

Going back to computers or more specifically home computers, the rapid advancement of these were originally fuelled by the want for businesses to allow their staff to work from home, and as the demand increased the price came down and the range got bigger. IBM, Commodore and Amstrad were the front runners to begin with but they aimed their systems to the business market. Finally, someone saw the gaping chasm that was the home education market. The skill was to market these to the parents as an aid to help the child with their education. The first break in the market was the BBC Microcomputer made by Acorn computers. This robust and stylish unit had a full sized QWERTY keyboard with additional keys for different functions. There were even educational television programs by the BBC aimed directly at teaching children (and some adults) how to use their computer for practical purposes.

Thus the first systems came with word processing and data-base software and stored their data on external floppy discs (the first ones were actually a little floppy). But these computers were still expensive options and either out of reach of parent's wallets, or not deemed worthy of the expense. What was needed was a system that was affordable, had the ability to word process and calculate, and to store information for future use. Enter the Sinclair ZX81.

A small but beautifully designed lump of plastic about the size of an exercise book. It wasn't really designed as a working tool and you would have struggled to convince any parent with their finger on the button (no pun intended) that it would be used for your homework. Its keyboard had no actual keys to press instead it had a membrane which you had to sort of gently push down to operate. However, it did have the selling feature of being affordable, around £70, and was well marketed as the item that would turn your child into the next Alan Turing. You see, what was possible on this tiny unassuming black box was the ability to write your own programs, to design your own software for whatever purpose you needed. This, primarily due to the basic features and limited memory (1kb) ultimately came down to games, which in turn were very basic. Can you even imagine anything working with 1kb of memory? If you were looking to play space invaders like the ones in the arcades you were going to be more than a little disappointed. There was no colour, the graphics were just black blocks that you had to clump together to make a shape, and there was no sound. Not much to go on but this tiny unit changed mine, and tens of thousands of others life.

Back then when I first laid fingers on to the computer I wasn't expecting it to give me that quality of gaming I played in the arcades (okay, I was hoping), I was looking to learn something, to do something with it. Like many things looking back it's very difficult to give an analogy to modern technology. With mobile phones we're so used to loading new apps every day that anything new isn't that much of a surprise and the excitement doesn't last long. Imagine if you can, getting your first ever touch screen mobile phone, trying to find out what all the little features and nuances it has and what you can do with them. Hold on to that thought as that first glimpse of something new is the best way to describe the feeling when I was first introduced to the ZX81. But for me there was nothing before to compare with, nothing to guide me on what I could do with it, and to other degree's what I couldn't do with it.

To help feed this insatiable appetite for more, magazines started to hit the newsagent's shelves dedicated to the new technology with reviews of the latest games, along with listings of programs and games that you make yourself. This did involve quite some work on your part as you had to laboriously and carefully type in the program from the pages, ensuring every dot and dash were correctly entered, a task made all the harder with the membrane keyboard. It could take hours, meticulously checking that all the spelling was correct and the relevant commas and punctuation marks were in the right place and also ensuring the computer wasn't knocked around too much, especially if the 16k ram pack was fitted as this could spell disaster as the computer would crash and you would have to start over again. Eventually after completing the typing it needed to be saved for future use. This is where the C15 cassette tapes I mentioned earlier come in to place.

As it was important to keep the cost of the system down, software was stored on to cassette tapes rather than the expensive disc option. The cassette recorder would be plugged in to the computer via the headphone/microphone socket. A very simple program of maybe no more than a couple of pages of data could take up to 5 minutes to save, and that might not even work. You see, these were temperamental machines, any little nudge or tap would be enough to wreck the recording, but you would not know until you tried to load it afterwards. The fault might also lay with the magazine's typing error which you would not find out until a correction and apology appeared in the next week's issue. There was a small advantage of typing these lists in to the computer, and that was the fact you were 'learning' to programme. The computer language that gave you this access was called BASIC, which I pride myself in remembering stands for, Beginners All-purpose Symbolic Instructional Code. You can see why they made it an acronym.

All these issues were not confined to the Sinclair range of computers. All of the manufacturers of the early home computing era had similar limitations if they were to keep their prices competitive. The next stage of machines moved forward to faster processors leading to colour graphics, sound and more realistic keyboards. The ZX81 paved the way for machines such as the Sinclair Spectrum, Commodore 64, Dragon 32, Jupiter Ace, Acorn Atmos to name but a few. The market was saturated with these competing machines, and unfortunately many of these models quickly fell by the wayside and left Sinclair and Commodore as the two behemoths to slug it out for first place much like Sega and Nintendo did in the 90's. For what it's worth I fell squarely down on the Spectrum side, which was probably due to loyalty to the Sinclair brand from owning the ZX81. There were many differences between each machine; one out weighing the other in differing areas but it's fair to say, much like your favourite football team, which ever machine you owned you stood by it.

Supplies of games, and I say games as by then there was very little use in trying to sell the machines as educational devices, created a new style of High Street retailer, the computer stores. Dedicated stores aimed squarely at the young burgeoning market that was growing rapidly with the advancement of these machines. Our local store had shelves upon shelves of brightly coloured cassette tapes, sectioned off for your particular computer and prices that were just within the reach a school kid could afford, but much like a kid in a sweet shop it was difficult to decide which one to plumb for. But if you couldn't decide or the game was out of your financial reach there was another, slightly dodgy option. The school playground became the black market where games, or should I say copies of games, swapped around like Top Trump cards or football stickers. I'm not condoning the concept of software piracy and I suppose looking back on it I feel a little guilty of participating in such an activity. However, if I wanted to play the range of games available, the market was there. I did purchase lots of games with my brother so my conscience is a little clearer, even if these games were later traded for others.

These early next generation home computers were capable of more than just games, they were in their own right a 'proper' computer. Basic as they were, they could run word processing, data base and art programmes and more importantly they allowed you to program them. Granted they weren't a patch on today's Apple's and PC's but they lead the way and without these machines I'm not sure where the computer industry would be now. It is quite plausible to say that a lot of today's computer boffins and games creators cut their teeth on machines like these. Personally the fact that the machines played games swung me away from the programming side which in hindsight was not the best move, computer programmers today can earn a decent amount of money. Oh well, at least I got to play Donkey Kong at home.

There were possibilities to play more realistic arcade games in your home prior to the invention of the home computer. One of the earliest forms of games consoles was the Atari Video Computer System, a brown wooden-veneer effect box (see, I told you there was a theme) which had a slot on the top for cartridges, much like the Nintendo NES and Sega Mega Drive did later on in the 90's. These were still basic machines in comparison to the giants of home entertainment we have today. The control system was not a joy pad but a joystick or paddle as the requirements of most of the games had very little more than up, down, side to side and fire. The colour and image resolution was way below what most of today's children would expect from a games machine, but then it didn't need to be with the style of games played. A revolution in home entertainment, this console, despite not appearing to come from the future due to its ability to blend in with the other oak effect furniture, paved the way for the onslaught of the big aforementioned names. Games started to resemble and emulate their bigger arcade cousins. No longer did you have to nag your parents to go to the nearest seaside resort in order to throw your pocket money into the latest amusement arcade. Of course, as with the home computers these units required a television for use which had the tendency to create 'issues' with the big people in the house. Compromises were struck, mainly weighted heavily in the parent's favour, giving the small people some time regulated use during weekends and some evenings in exchange for household chores, but this was enough to start with. After a while benefits arrived for both parties as the cost of portable TV's became affordable and the spare room became the dedicated games room. I recall my first TV being a very old black and white portable that my dad used to have as an emergency backup if the main television broke. I think he originally got it as it could be powered by a car battery and was to be used when we went away. It never was. But it became our first games dedicated screen and as the ZX81 only had black and white graphics it didn't really matter about the colour; that was the next revolutionary step.

The Sinclair Spectrum and the Commodore 64 became the next battleground of home computers. They had more memory, 48k with the Spectrum and as you could probably guess 64k with the Commodore. They were also quite different in appearance; the Commodore had a proper keyboard which made it look more professional and grown up. The Spectrum however maintained the unique styling its predecessor had, small black unit but this time with rubber keyboard. Each machine had its pros and cons but as with the previous incarnations you stuck by your manufacturer of choice. A little known fact but the Commodore 64 has sold more units than any other personal computer, approximately up to 17 million from 1982 to 1994.

The big difference between these and their predecessors was the inclusion of colour and sound. I recall the first time we loaded the Spectrum, it came with an introductory cassette which had a few demos on it. As it was our new colour computer we used the opportunity of a Saturday morning to connect it up to the colour TV in the living room. Whilst loading the game the edge of the screen flashed a multitude of colours in a random order and the cassette bleeped and screeched to inform you something was happening. What happened next was jaw dropping excitement for me and my brother, the screen unveiled a large image of a planet, not dissimilar to Saturn with the company logo (Psion) emblazoned across it. Amazing. There were flaws, obviously, again much to do with the reliability of the loading of games, the volume had to be just right, too loud or to quiet made all the difference. The keys might not always react as quick as you'd like, the colours on the screen often clashed and the sound was quite bleepy, but from what we had before it was the best thing since a loaf of bread and a knife were introduced to each other. There are numerous games of that period that stand out as being game changers (pun definitely intended), Jet Set Willy, Lunar Jetman, Dizzy, Sabrewolf and many, many more. I've listed some of my favourite and popular iconic games at the end of this chapter.

So, what about portable machines akin to today's Nintendo Game-boys and Sony PS Vita I hear you say? Well there were some handheld devices but I would be hard pressed to call them games consoles. In essence they were pocket sized devices which had an LCD screen within which would be black and white or more specifically black graphics on top of the grey screen background. The game play was very limited; a football game for example would have a basic image, similar to a digital watch of a footballer who could only move to three positions, the main skill of the game would be timing, not accuracy as that was already pre-determined. However, these simple and compact games kept us quiet for long enough for the bus journey home or the waiting period before tea.

The main arcade game of this era was Space Invaders; you couldn't pass an amusement arcade without hearing the now iconic bleeps and explosions the machines made. A trip to the seaside didn't happen that often so we had to get our kick another way. I've mentioned the LCD pocket games as they were truly pocket games but didn't satisfy our need for arcade realism, but there were number of new options on the market.

Small (ish) games machines became popular, handheld devices which gave you the chance to shoot and kill as many aliens you could before you ran out of lives. Improvements in technology replaced the old LCD graphics with bright and colourful LED's. These varied in size and quality, the better ones being the slightly larger units which gave the aliens further to fall before you wiped them out. Probably one of the classic and, for me anyway, more memorable was Grandstands Astro Wars. It had a proper joystick and large fire button, a choice of levels and speeds, and at the end of each level you slowly built a rocket ship with the culmination of the end sequence when it launched and disappeared off the top of the screen. Again this wasn't directly a hand held unit, it had a mains adapter but could also work on batteries, but it gave the option to play Space Invaders at home.

Fast forward to 2016 and the changes are phenomenal. Nintendo DS and Sony PSP to name but a few with their plug in cartridge games, high definition and touch screens and long life batteries are a world apart from thirty years ago. Even these now are being replaced by mobile phone and tablet computers with hundreds of apps and games available at a swipe of a screen. Interestingly from my point of view is that a lot of the games are 'retro' games of old which prove that the games of the eighties were the best ever, and that is obviously fact. I think at this point it's worth giving you some examples of the sort of games that I and others like me played at the dawn of this new computer age. These are by no means the best or worst that were produced, there were plenty of bad ones, but these are some of the ones I played.

Jet Set Willy – ZX Spectrum 1984

Probably one of the most iconic and well-remembered Spectrum games of all time, a sequel to Manic Miner, a classic game in itself. Designed by the legendary Matt Smith and distributed by Software Projects, it was a platform game but not quite like the ones we know today. The premise was that Mr Willy (it was never revealed whether it was his first name or surname), had to tidy up all the items left around his house after a huge party. With this done his housekeeper Maria will allow him access to his bedroom. Willy's mansion was bought with the wealth obtained from his adventures in 'Manic Miner' but much of it remains unexplored and it appears to be full of strange creatures. Willy must explore the enormous 61 roomed mansion and its grounds (including a beach and a yacht) to fully tidy up the house so he can get some much-needed sleep. Willy was controlled by simple left, right or jump buttons but unlike most of the standard platform games you weren't stuck to completing each screen before moving on to the next, you could walk through, or rather jump through each level to get to the next room, and if you wanted to go backwards. Many rooms, just like a real mansion had more than one door in or out which would then lead you to another room etc. One of the computer magazines of the time

43

created a map of the whole building cleverly designed to look like a mansion which was of great help in navigating around the huge game. There were of course ways to cheat should you so desire, specific key presses and pokes (pokes are a series of numbers entered which alters the game code) which would give you unlimited life or even take you to the end screen but majority of the time it was more fun trying to win without resorting to such low levels.

All in all JSW is a game that I remember fondly and will always remind me of my early days of gaming.

Lunar Jetman – ZX Spectrum 1983

Imagine being in a space suit with a jet pack, a laser gun and a moon buggy. Imagine all this and being trapped on an alien world, your mission to destroy alien bases whilst defending yourself against the flying inhabitants and flaming meteors intent on your destruction. Got that? Well that's the predicament Lunar Jetman found himself in this all-time favourite game. To make the game more interesting your jetpack had a limited amount of fuel and when this ran out you had to walk the distance to your moon buggy which would refuel your jetpack and give you protective cover from the meteors and aliens. To blow up the bases you had to drop a bomb over them which could be taken to the base in two ways; firstly by picking it up and flying to the base and releasing your payload, but with limited fuel that was a tough ask. Second and much more sensible option was to put the bomb on the back of the buggy and drive to the base then taking it off and carrying out your deadly deed. However, the buggy could only travel on flat surfaces and wouldn't you know it, the moon is not flat. You had to build bridges over the craters in order to continue your drive. This game was definitely one of the best Spectrum games visually and the addictiveness of the game-play left you wanting to go back for more. If you want to see how a good game was made on a limited amount of memory and graphics you would struggle to find many better examples.

Match Day 2 – ZX Spectrum 1987

We are so used to realistic football games on the X-Box and Playstation that anything less than realism is sneered at, so this might be a tough sell. Match Day 2 was the follow up to the successful Match Day (no prizes for originality in the title), one of the most 'realistic' football games with a game play that for the time emulated the beautiful game on screen. There were some obvious omissions due to the constraints of the machine; there were only 7 players per team, no sliding tackles, no off-sides and no cards but it didn't detract from the game itself. The pitch was viewed from the side line and had the lines converging further up the screen to give an element of perspective. Four keys were used to control the player's directions with a separate one to shoot and jump, even heading the ball was included. Games could be played against the computer but more fun was had player another person, however the small keyboard of the Spectrum made it quite tight getting all the fingers on the right keys. There were glitches as could be expected particularly that if your opponent pressed a key it may make your player shoot early giving the ball away. Game play was slow but again you accepted that and got on with it. 'When the Saints go marching in' was played as the players came out onto the pitch and a shrill whistle kicked the game off. Admittedly this game falls past the remit of the book as it was released in 1987 but it's predecessor was released in 1984. It's just that I consider this to be the better game so it's in the list and that's that.

Match Point – ZX Spectrum 1984

Tennis is a difficult game to replicate on a computer. The dynamics of the balls movements; topspin, slice, back spin, lob and volley not to mention the players' movements all require a large degree of programming to get right so to do this on the limited memory and graphics capability of the Spectrum is outstanding. Match Point manages this perfectly while retaining game play and speed. Graphically it's nothing astounding, the court is pretty much as expected with the far end of the court narrowing to give a good perspective. The players were even less outstanding; they looked very similar to the men depicted on the road side signs but to their credit their movement was swift and smooth, and the tennis racquet moved smoothly from hand to hand. Amazingly some of the strokes were possible, drop shots over the net, lobs and smashes were all there and created excellent options to your game. If you look at the screen shot of this game it doesn't give you much encouragement to load it and play but if you did you would be hooked. Sure it's not Pete Sampras or Andy Murray but it certainly has great gameplay and that's what counts. It's most definitely a worthy addition to my all-time top ten Spectrum games.

Daley Thompson Decathlon – ZX Spectrum 1984

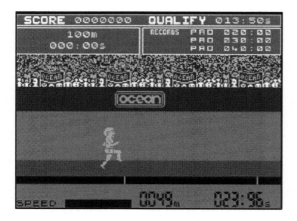

Daley Thompson was an iconic athlete in the early 1980's achieving gold medals at 2 Olympic Games, 1980 and 1984 as well as breaking the world record numerous times in the decathlon, so it would be only right to create a computer game based around his success. Unlike many games that are spun off from the success of a film, this game was a pretty good and respectful attempt and gave the player opportunities to compete in all ten events. The game was also known for helping the joystick market in sales as the game required a lot of joystick waggling. Effectively the game involved tapping the keyboard or waggling the joystick as fast as possible to make Daley run as fast as possible. For the events that required more than just running, timing was of the essence. Pressing the jump/throw key had to be timed to perfection or it would lead to a foul jump or a spectacular collapse in the case of the pole vault. Graphically it was fairly simple, all the action being a side on view with a simple stadium backdrop and Daley not looking anything like the main man himself. It was a game I kept going back to and was worthy of the 5 minutes waiting for it to load.

Skool Daze / Back to Skool – ZX Spectrum 1984

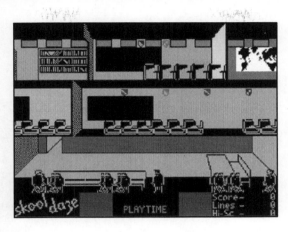

Quite a different style of game this, a side on view of a school building cut so you could see all the classrooms, staff and pupils inside. You controlled the main character Eric, whose task was to steal his report card from the staff room safe by means of knocking all the shields on the walls which gave you a letter, eventually leading to the password for the safe. As you would expect in any self-respecting school there was a school bully who you'd do well to avoid. Although devoid of the use of a catapult he dispenses his cruelty with the equally effective punch. In your defence you could also punch him and the other kids or knock him down with a well aimed catapult shot. If you felt like being even more rebellious you could knock down a teacher but make sure you're not around when he gets up or you'll get lines, too many lines and the game would end with Eric getting expelled from the school. Back to Skool was a sequel that offered a similar role and removed some glitches that were present in Skool Daze. The games certainly weren't a true reflection of my school childhood, for example catapults were not allowed even then. The game seemed to be modelled around the likes of Just William or the Bash Street Kids from the Beano. As I said a different type of 'platform' style games and one that made it worth going to skool for!

Ant Attack – ZX Spectrum 1983

The title suggests an all-out blast fest; first person shooter like Call of Duty or similar shoot and kill games. Nothing however could be further from the truth. There were ants involved, giant ants to be precise and they went about their business in a 3-dimensional brick walled 'city'. Just like a scene from a 1920's black and white movies there was a girl in distress who needed rescuing. She wasn't tied to a railway track and there was no villain twisting his moustache, she was in fact stuck in some part of the wall or on lump of bricks in the centre of the compound. I say she but it was also possible to have the hero as a girl and to rescue a dumb bloke. To help them in their cause to free the hostage and avoid getting bitten by the ants you had an arsenal of hand grenades you could throw which didn't kill the ants, more stunned them for a while. Although only in black and white the game had a three-dimensional effect, or isometric as it is formally known, which allowed the player to spin the city around to see all four sides, essential as quite often the damsel/fools would be hidden behind a wall. A simple yet addictive game that kept me amused on many long winter nights.

Atic Atac – ZX Spectrum 1983

Ultimate were a prolific software developer of the 80's and were responsible for a number of high quality games. Atic Atac is one of them. The premise is fairly simple; find all the pieces of the golden key hidden in the castle to win. But of course it was more than just running through rooms until you find it, there were creatures and objects ready and waiting to drain you of your precious health, the lack of which would eventually kill you. And when you did die a gravestone would rise from the ground and remain throughout the game to remind you of your failures in a previous life. To regain your strength roast chickens would be placed randomly around the castle although they could only be eaten once so had to be used sparingly. A nice touch of the game was that it allowed you to select a character at the beginning; a wizard, knight or serf each one having access to certain doors but not others. So for example you could be in a room with three doors but if you were a knight could only go through one, if you were another character a different door would be open to you but would lead to a different room. Door keys are scattered around the rooms, most are essential to open certain colour coded doors and the rooms may contain another useful item needed for another part of the castle. The game was complex and the castle seemed huge, one of the computer magazines printed a map of the castle to help out those who needed it much like they did for Jet Set Willy. An absolute classic game and as it could be played with three different characters effectively made it sort of three in one, or maybe not, but it definitely deserves a place in my list of all-time favourites.

Death Chase – ZX Spectrum 1983

A strange game this and definitely not one for epileptics. Talking of which I don't ever recall any warning messages on games as you see on all modern console games which is even more unusual as the due to the limited range of colours games then had much more flashing images than today. The concept of this game is to control a motorcyclist as he pursues two other motorcycles, one blue and one yellow, through a multi coloured forest. The bike is equipped with guns which are used to destroy the other bikes which when fired the bullets can be steered by turning the bike left or right, obviously still dodging the oncoming trees. There are night time levels and every now and then helicopters and tanks appear in the distance, hitting them gains extra points. As I said the Spectrum had limited colours which resulted in many of the trees being purple in colour, but at least the grass was green and sky blue as you would hope. A decent and addictive game although due to the fast flashing colours of the trees passing by it's one that was likely to give you eyestrain and a headache if played too long.

The Hobbit – ZX Spectrum 1982

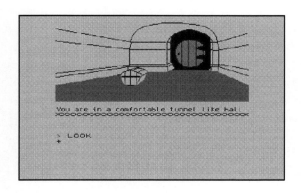

The Hobbit as I'm sure you're aware is an adventure book written by J.R.R.Tolkein and follows the adventures of Bilbo Baggins as he searches for a stash of treasure guarded by Smaug the dragon. In the game you play the part of our would-be hero sending him off to find his riches. As a text based adventure you controlled

Bilbo by certain commands, 'pick up key', 'go east', 'open door' and similar phrases. As you enter a new room or area a message will give you an idea of what you can see. 'You are in a small room, to the east is a round green door, you can see a wooden chest'. Although it was a text based game as you entered a new screen a line drawing relating to that part of the games would be drawn, which was a little slow at times depending on the picture. The problem with this and other text based adventures is that the programme would only respond to directions correctly typed, the type of smart word recognition we now have in Google searches were a long way away. So for example if you see a green door to the east typing 'open door' would not suffice, 'open green door' might have worked or even 'open the green door'. When you eventually get the computer to recognise what you want it to do it would probably come back and tell you that the green door is locked!!

All this makes it sound like the most annoying game ever, and it probably was but it led the way for many other adventure games, and importantly for an early teenager it also allowed us to type rude words and commands. The other characters in the game had full autonomy and could roam the Tolkien world freely, possibly disrupting your advancement by breaking an object you need or killing another character that you needed to help you with another part of the adventure later on. This could lead to the premise of not being able to complete the game. Although some of these errors were fixed in later updates but I don't think it was ever fully bug free. So why is this in my top list of Spectrum games? It's simply because it was the first adventure game I had played and whilst frustrating I kept going back for more hoping that at some point I could get through that green door!

Stonkers – ZX Spectrum – 1983

How do I describe Stonkers? It's not an action game, or a first person shooter, it's more of a strategy game, think of the board game Risk and you'll be somewhere near the idea. You take charge of an army with the sole aim of destroying the other computer controlled enemy. At your command are tanks, artillery and infantry which also need to be supplied with ammunition and food in order to continue its advance on the enemy lines. These are delivered by supply trucks that are themselves supplied by ships. Timing was crucial, an army marches on its stomach and without continued supply your protagonists would starve and die. Each unit can be sent into battle but you could only move them one at a time which led it to being quite a long game. Graphically it was nothing ground breaking, in fact it was a static screen of a map of some fictitious land, and it was a slow game, again akin to Risk, the only moving part being your figures and a ticker tape at the bottom of the screen giving you up to date information about your troops.

Another one of those 'why is this in the list' games and I sort of agree but it's its unique game play, the strategy of battle and the simplicity that sent me back for more, or maybe I just like war games.

No doubt I've missed out plenty of games that you may have played, and let's face it there are plenty of them. 'What about Manic Miner, or Monty Mole or Chuckie Egg' I hear you say, well these are all fantastic games and I would include them in my all-time favourites. However, that would make this a book of computer games, if that's what you want than there are plenty of books on the market that will give lists of computer games around during this time; it's worth looking out for them. But this is not one of them.

Chapter 4

Fun and games

In the absence of the modern world of Playstation, X-Box and other games machines fun was found in many other ways. Now let me start by stating that many of the pastimes I'm about to talk about are still around and are played by children today, but they have been steadily replaced by the aforementioned modern technology. During the early to mid-seventies indoor entertainment was very much based around board and card games. The traditional and still popular games such as Monopoly, Ker-Plunk, and draughts were a staple diet of evening 'family' fun time, and I can't stress enough the word family in that sentence. Many an evening was spent with my siblings and parents crouched over a board or playing cards competing to win the pile of pennies on the floor. Ok, you could argue that this was also an early introduction to gambling but was never viewed as such, it was just healthy competition. That said, those pennies would buy a lot of sweets back then so maybe there was some gambling involved.

During the early 70's there were industrial strikes which lead to power cuts rendering the brown box in the corner surplus to requirements. We are so used to the world lit up by artificial light that I'm sure most of us would find it quite disorientating to be so quickly slammed in to the dark. Candles which were standard cupboard items were lit and everyone congregated into the living room huddled around a table lit only by candles (wax ones, not these new paraffin tea lights), large flickering shadows dancing on the walls and a small smell of burning from the wick of the candles created a magical atmosphere. Many households still had open fires which eased some of the lighting issues, at least for the living room anyway. We had only recently moved in to a new council house devoid of such natural means of heat and light, natures very own TV as my Mum used to say. Without the candles, as you would expect it was dark, very dark, not only because the house lights were out but also the street lights that would normally seep through the curtains were powerless. Of course today we would still have lights from our mobile phones or tablets but back then there wasn't such gizmo's, torch and candle were the only means of illumination. I recall we also had paraffin based light, a glass cylinder with a mesh type wick in the centre. The base would be filled with Paraffin and a chrome pump handle was used to get the flammable liquid to its desired location. A match ignited the flame and the glass cover was placed back. A little dial (I keep telling you) used to increase the brightness of the flame. Although the overriding memory is of the smell of burning fuel that permutated around the house, no doubt it would fall foul of the Health & Safety brigade today, but at least we had light.

Heating would also go off as even gas boilers need a spark of electricity to get them going. We would sit wrapped up in our warm clothing in the living room with enough candles to guide a ship in to port, a paraffin lamp and a card game on the go. So winter nights were cold and dark but in some ways warm and comforting. All of a sudden the power came on without much warning and if you'd left the lights on you would be instantly blinded for a few seconds by the return of the modern world. The candles were extinguished and put aside for another night, and the game could continue without any risk of eye strain or calling the fire brigade. But I was always quite sad when the power came back, it was exciting and mystical and strange all at the same time and when the 20th Century came back in all its splendour, that moment was lost. But if you didn't have anyone to play board games with, or more over they didn't want to play with you there was still solace to be found in small plastic figurines. Toy soldiers, Cowboys and Indians or toy cars were a child's way of leaving the world of reality for a while and joining the world of imagination. Wars between different factions of figures could be arranged with the outcome more or less pre-set as you always had your favourite action figure. Toy cars would have a life and personality of their own, much like Disney's film Cars. Thinking about that I wonder if I can sue them on the grounds of artistic infringement, might be worth a bob or two or I'll happily settle out of court, just a thought.

Anyway, if toy soldiers weren't your thing there were other solitary pastimes; Etch-a-sketch could keep you happy for a while, even if it meant just drawing circles and squares. I didn't know anyone who could draw some of the pictures on the cover of the box. Most of the time I spent trying to scribe my name, but with some letters it was necessary to go over the same line twice without looking obvious. Not that easy on curved letters.

Spirograph looked like a school science kit. It had a plethora of different shaped plastic pieces with ridges around the edge and holes in the centre; a protractor wouldn't have looked out of place in the box. Select one of the shapes, a circle for example and pin it onto a piece of paper (preferably on top of some card board to protect the dining room table). Hold another of the plastic shapes on to the circle; insert a pencil and using the cogs slowly move it around the centre piece, and a pattern should appear. Change the outside piece to another different shape and

59

repeat. The results are quite effective and if you use different coloured pencils can be quite psychedelic, however the 'game' did have a limited appeal, after all Mum could only fit so many colourful pictures on the fridge.

Airfix kits were popular especially for boys as they tended to be vehicles of war; tanks, battleships and aeroplanes being the mainstay although popular cars and motorbikes also featured heavily in the available packs. I would happily spend hours if not days meticulously constructing and painting a Spitfire only at a later stage attach it to some string hung from the bedroom widow down to the garden fence, letting go and hoping that my brother would catch it at the bottom. I remember once we taped some paper to it, lit it and let it go as if it had been shot down, then using a magnifying glass using the Sun that was always out in summer, burning holes in to the bodywork to simulate bullet holes. They seemed to be a present given to a child of a certain age when it was difficult to buy things for, after this stage it came down to music vouchers, one small step away from getting just a card.

If playing card games for pennies wasn't enough of an introduction to gambling, why not try this excellent board game. 'Lose your shirt' was a game based around horse racing, the aim is pretty explanatory, make as much money as you can. It came with a thick green roll of cloth, similar to a snooker table cloth with a grid marked on it. 6 coloured plastic horses, a pack of action cards and some pretend cash. Each card had an instruction, move forward one square, move back two, move sideward's and so on. At the beginning of the game you chose secretly which horse to back and carefully use your cards try to and ensure you get your horse to the finishing line first. Betting odds allow you to go for broke and put all your money on one horse or give an even split and have more chance of winning small amounts. I'm not sure this review is giving it as much credit as it deserves as it was a cracking game.

Fuzzy Felt was a piece of cardboard around twice the size of an A4 piece of paper with one side covered in felt. The colour of this felt varied according to the theme the contents related to, for example a summer scene would be yellow, a circus would be green and a space scene would be blue, you get the idea. Inside the box would be cut out shapes made from felt relating to the theme. I remember having a circus theme which contained sea lions, beach balls, coloured arms and legs and other odd shapes from which I was supposed to make an attractive and life like scene. It never happened. The science behind Fuzzy Felt was simple; felt stuck to felt, well sort of, but enough to keep the pieces on the board. The problem was more kits were needed to give you a greater chance of creating any type of scene other than that of the kit provided. But as a new box of Fuzzy Felt may cost the same as a new board game there was only ever going to be one winner. The pieces would slowly go missing in the same way odd socks go missing in the washing machine, never to be seen again until eventually you were left with a piece of cardboard with felt on one side and the odd circle or triangle to stick to it. All the same it was quite good fun in my early years, but I don't think I'll be searching E-Bay any time soon.

When the lights went out during the power cuts in the early 70's we would play cards, but sometimes we would play Frustration. This game featured a brilliant way of ensuring the dice did not get lost; they put the dice in to a plastic dome in the centre of the board. But this was no ordinary plastic dome; this was a 'pop-o-matic' dome. When the dome was pressed and then released it gave two clunk sounds and the dice bounced around inside due to a spring system underneath the dome. It was a simple idea of throwing dice without actually throwing them. The game is still going strong and has been updated for the modern age. I know this game, and 'Lose your shirt' aren't solo games but they were part of the fun had on an evening before bedtime.

If all these games were too much bother to get out, set up, lose bits, find the bits and then put the game away there was always the go to solo activity; comics. Comics were a weekly purchase and the beauty of having siblings was all of us had our own favourite comics, so we all had three different comics to read each week. I know in the early years I used to get the Beano with all its regular characters, Denis the Menace, Minie the Minx, Bash Street Kids, Roger the Dodger and my favourite Billy Whizz, but I also recall the Dandy being around the house as Desperate Dan and Bully Beef and Chips were a regular read. But it was in the late 70's that the two comics I recall waiting to get were released. 'Krazy' was a sort of anarchic comic full of totally different strips and just seemed, to a young boy anyway, that bit more edgy. The 12 ½ p Buytonic Boy was probably one of the better remembered strips. Based upon the TV series 'The Bionic Man', it followed the exploits of a kid called Steve Ford who bought a tonic drink from a strange man in the street and gained super hero powers. I think the less said about the practice of buying from strangers in the street, no matter how cheap it is, the better. After a while one of the 'Krazy' gang went off to create his own self-styled comic. 'Cheeky' was a goofy lad who walked through the comic in between the normal comic strips commenting and making relevant jokes as he went along. His pet snail (this is a kid's comic so anything goes) would slide around the margins and although he couldn't speak we could see his thoughts in a think bubble. Many an afternoon was spent in the bedroom reading the comics and munching through penny sweets like Black Jacks, Rhubarb and Custard and Drumsticks. Some of these penny sweets only cost half pence so you'd get two for the price of one. Penny sweets don't seem to exist anymore, or rather they don't cost a penny and half pence coins went out the window in the early eighties. On that subject I could happily drone on about the size of Wagon Wheels and Mars bars being much bigger then than they are now, or name lots of sweets that have ceased to exist in all but memories but there are hundreds of books that do that in a lot more detail. I still find myself saying Marathon instead of Snickers and Opal Fruits instead of Starbursts, old habits die hard.

There was of course the option to play 'outside', a concept that seems a little strange to some kids of today. I don't mean that as a generalisation, there are plenty kids who entertain themselves in the big open world, but not as many as I suspect. Obviously for a boy the appeal of a game of footie was a big enough lure to get me outside no matter what was on TV. Groups of us from different parts of the estate would meet on the school playing field, not planned just turned up at what seemed to be the time to play football. Teams would be unevenly split with the older kids choosing their team leaving the kids who only turned because they had nothing better to do and had no idea about football. If you were good and showed your skill, or a turn of pace you would be deemed good enough to be picked for the first team next time, which I brazenly brag is where I fitted in. I was small but fast and I was a decent football player to grab the odd moment of glory. If only a keen football scout would have been passing by at the right time who knows what could have happened?

Plenty of other outside activities apart from climbing trees and riding bikes were games such as Block 1-2-3 which was basically hide and seek. It may have been called something different in other areas of the country but for the purposes of this book it was called Block 1-2-3. We played games that are probably outlawed now or considered violent and disruptive like British Bulldog; a large group of kids running at one trying to avoid being caught. If you were caught you would join this lonely figure and help him catch more eventually being more catchers than runners. A good old rough and tumble game where injuries were common place.

If we were bored or just felt like being mischievous we would play 'Knock off ginger' a basic practice of knocking on someone's door and running away to a safe hiding place where you still view the door and its disgruntled owner. I know this game is called different things in different parts of the country and why it's called knock off ginger where I lived is a mystery, we might just have called it knock, run and hide but where's the mystery in that? A really mischievous version of the game was to balance a milk bottle on to the handle and then knock and run and watch the obvious consequences of our actions. I will say now that I don't condone my actions but merely state that I was just a follower of the boys who did this and that obviously, I cleaned up the mess later on. Honest.

Chapter 5

Communication

Another big topic, where do I begin? I find it difficult to live without my mobile phone. My wife says I break out into a cold sweat if I'm more than ten feet away from it which is unfair, I can manage at least fifteen. But it's not just a phone; it is a small portable computer capable of sending and receiving emails, a diary, a games machine, a TV and a camera all in a box that fits neatly into the palm of a hand.

We have become so reliant on these devices in the last ten years that our lives stop if we can't check it every ten minutes of the day just to see that no-one has contacted us. How many of us actually use them to call people? I haven't done a lot of research in to this, actually I haven't done any, but the point is more and more people are using them to contact friends via text, Facebook or other social media sites. Of course I use the term 'friends' in brackets as I don't believe for one minute those who have 100+ friends on these social media sites have ever met them all. Either way, this is yet again another form of science fiction that in the seventies we really couldn't have even dreamt would become reality. Back then most households didn't even have a house telephone let alone a mobile, instead there were public telephones dotted around the main streets for use by all and sundry. This was sometimes pointless as friends and family also had no telephone so there was only a small amount of occasions they were used. The phones in the booths had a slot for coins, 10 pence being the order of the day, so to make a call you had to have a bag full of coins if you were expecting a lengthy conversation. The phone booths were also used for unsolicited advertising, but the adverts were not something you would want children to read, and they were also used by the odd late night reveller as an emergency facility.

So how on earth did we keep in touch? Well firstly we didn't have 'friends' who we'd never met before (and probably not likely to), we tended to have a closer knit group of friends and family, some of which we went to school with, some were friends of friends but majority were the ones who lived nearby, down the street, across the road or even next door. As I was only a small boy I did not use the telephone box very often, but it was a common sight to see them in use during the day, possibly for calling taxi's etc.

Eventually late in the 1970's we received our first telephone; a smooth rounded grey box with a darker coloured handle attached by a coiled cable and in the centre of the front face a dial. You see, I keep telling you they're the future. The dial had the obvious numbers 1 to 0 covered by a clear disc with finger holes which you used to dial the number. One of the most memorable features of these phones is the sound they made when you dialled a number. A sound that I can guarantee would make anyone from that era smile wistfully with remembrance. I did find an App recently that mimicked the dial action and sound which is worth downloading just for the nostalgia but not quite the same as the tactile feel of the original. What has always baffled me is why the number 9, the one you would need to use three times in an emergency, was the last number on the ring. If ever there was a time you needed to call someone quickly it was in an emergency. A space in the house was dedicated to the telephone and a new piece of furniture was added to the dusting list for Mum, the telephone table. Handily located at the bottom of the stairs, or sometimes in the space under the stairs, this new furniture comprised of a leather effect seat with a small shelf at one end upon which the telephone would reside. Underneath the shelf would be space to store the telephone directory, a list of telephone numbers and addresses of everyone in the local area. Useful as this was, you would know off by heart the number of all your friend and family, those that weren't that regularly used would be written on a sheet of paper attached to the wall or in the telephone index. The telephone index was akin to a file-o-fax in that it had tabs for each letter of the alphabet where you would store names and numbers to avoid getting out the phone book. These telephone pads came in different guises and ways of selecting the letter, from slides to levers to dials, available in all many of colours, fake wooden effect being the order of the day to match the table. And innovation didn't stop there; the next advancement was the trim phone, a flat oblong phone with a modern looking handset and push buttons that bleeped when you pressed them replaced the dials. Available in a multitude of garish colours this new phone replaced the traditional bell for the ring tone with a screeching high pitch electronic noise. If you had one of these, you were definitely in a household set for the future. But as always there were drawbacks to this new household gadget, at the time there weren't enough telephone lines to cover all the houses wishing to become part of this new connected world. In order to alleviate this problem, the GPO would share lines with other users; a party line. Unfortunately, there was no party involved in sharing a telephone line with someone else, when you wanted to use the phone there was a good chance that the other user would be deep in conversation already. It was possible to gently lift the receiver and eavesdrop on the other conversation but bearing that in mind they could also do the same to you. Eventually more lines became available and the party was over.

The nearest thing I can recall that was considered mobile communication were 'walkie-talkie's'. These devices are still available today, some are aimed at the children's market and some are the top end of the range used by security firms when patrolling shopping centres and the like. The ones we had were more akin to the childrens version, though not pink or brightly coloured. These were designed to look like they were straight from a top secret military base. It failed. They were plastic, camouflage in colour and about the size and weight of a modern day selotape dispenser. A handy Morse-Code chart was stuck to the front of the panel for even more top secret communication. The weight was due to the large 'D' or 'C' sized batteries they used to power the unit which unfortunately did not have a great capacity and all too quickly died. They also had a very limited range and never quite as much as the advertisement on the box claimed. Twenty to thirty feet would be good, and it would be even better if you had a line of sight of the person on the other end! Admittedly these were not designed to operate much more than from one room to another so they needed a little bit of modification. I recall a friend who lived a few streets away suggesting we wire them up to a small CB radio aerial (more of that in a bit), and hoping to have the clarity of sound only available via telephone. We were somewhat disappointed. All we got was even more interference and static, the annoyance to my parents that it affected the TV signal and the only discernible advantage was the Morse code bleeps travelled further! All we needed now was to learn Morse code.

So the next stage of new world communication was the CB radio. Citizen Band radio had been around a long time in America and was used by long distance truckers to communicate to each other and was thrust into the UK limelight with films such as Convoy with its coded language. Who would have thought that a Rubber Duck and a Widow Woman would be ideal partners? Everyone wanted a ten four from all their 'good buddies' and were disappointed if an instant answer wasn't forth coming. So what was it all about?

I mentioned earlier about walkie-talkies and what they had to offer to the world of communication, CB radio was this concept and more. They weren't portable like the handheld walkie-talkies but had to remain fixed in place be it in the car, the bedroom or the garage, basically anywhere with mains power. Attached to the main unit via a coiled cable would be a handset with a nice big button on the side and to receive and send communication some sort of aerial was needed. These varied from a basic metal rod in the house, a massive pole attached to the outside of the house or for the car a lager wobbly aerial and for no apparent reason, usually fixed to the centre of the roof. The problem with the CB radio in the UK is that it used AM frequency airwaves which were not licensed for the UK market. Basically it was illegal in its current form. This didn't deter its popularity, in fact quite the opposite. As is always the case, if some form of entertainment is banned it generates more interest and consequently more people want to use it. When the BBC banned the playing of the song 'Relax' by Frankie Goes to Hollywood on its radio station in 1984 due to its possible explicit connotations, the single sold by the bucket load and went to number 1 in the music charts. But still the BBC refused to play it or even show it on Top of the Pops. A major coup for the band and one which made the band a household name, guaranteed to sell more singles. Would this have happened if it was not banned, probably not, and so the same happened with CB radio.

As the UK had had no allocation for such CB channels and therefore its use was illegal, people began importing America Citizens Band radios into the UK and the CB craze started. There were plusses and minuses for the system. It was free to call anyone and the initial layout for the radio and required accessories was fairly cheap in comparison to modern day mobile phones. However, the distance that could be reached varied between 5 to 10 miles with a standard home aerial although larger ones could easily double that. Having said that most of the people you would contact lived within the same town and generally within range. The radios were also able to be mounted in to the car giving access on the move, just like the truckers in the movies. However, as this was communication over the airwaves anyone could listen to your conversations so private chatter was not advised. But this problem also came with the advantage of having a group conversation, a feature not available on the telephone. The fun side of the hobby was the lingo, again brought over from the States but didn't quite sound the same within a northern accent. No-one used their real names, instead they gave themselves nicknames or 'handle's' as it was specifically known. So for example, if you wished to talk to a friend you would call out their handle not the real name. One Four 'Sexy Eyes', if the name of the person you desperately needed to speak to was called Sexy Eyes. One Four (14) was the number of the channel that was used for first contact. If someone replies telling you that she (let's presume it's a she for now even though men can also have sexy eyes) was not around, you didn't say thanks, oh no, you said ten four good buddy. It sounds a bit geeky, and in fact it was, but it was what it was, a free way of speaking to friends. Eventually the government legalised the system by allocating FM frequencies for use and the illegal AM declined, the fun being taken away now it was legal.

Of course there was the old fashioned way of communicating with people over a long distance; the letter. This may come as a shock to children of today but it was not uncommon to spend a short while writing, yes actually writing a letter in your finest handwriting giving the news and information you wanted to convey and of course asking questions about their life in the hope of receiving a reply. Pop it in an envelope and slot it onto the post box at the top of the street, which almost as a nod to the future tended to be sat next to the telephone box. A process of communication that hasn't changed for hundreds of years although with the advent of email, text and social media it has declined quite rapidly. I can't remember the last time I actually wrote a letter to a friend which is a great shame as the process was much more personal than a 5-word sentence with small pictures of smiling faces attached. Admittedly there was no instant response that is expected today but that wasn't what the activity was about, it was about the thought and consideration that went into the time writing, and in return the surprise of a letter on your own doormat when someone has reciprocated your thoughts. Also worth mentioning is the humble postcard. It is very much still around today and I for one always send one whilst away on my sojourns. Instead of taking a picture, uploading it to Facebook or other social media sites and letting the whole world know you're away from your home; we relied on these cards to let our friends see what a good time we were having, even if we weren't. The choices of cards were wide and varied from those with pictures of local main attractions, Stonehenge, Edinburgh Castle or the Arc de Triumph for example, to the cheeky seaside cards with the usual double entendre pictures and captions on the front. We could have phoned our family to let them know we were still away and lie to them how good the weather was, but if you've got a number of people to call the last thing you want to be doing on your holiday is to stand in a dirty and most definitely smelly telephone box shoving 10 pence's in by the minute. It's much easier, cheaper and more convenient to send a postcard.

Sadly, things have moved forward at pace. I say sadly because I think we are losing an art of communication that meant more to people when they received it. Handwritten letters, postcards, birthday cards are all slowly becoming extinct in favour of instant messaging and social media. Please don't get me wrong, I use texts and emails on a daily basis and find it an effective way of quick communication. I have still yet to be converted to the Facebook world, I'm not sure I could live with the fact that I only had a certain amount of 'friends' compared to others and the feeling that I was being followed all the time. I still find that if I want friends and family to see my holiday pictures I'll go and see them or email some of them, still that's sort of what this book is about, doing old fashioned tasks in the modern world.

We have come so far in what in essence is a short period of time. In the mid 90's we had our major breakthrough with mobile phone technology as Nokia, Motorola and Sony competed against each other and the newest form of retail outlet hit our high streets. Still fairly chunky (the phones, not the shops) and with limited capability they helped quench our thirst for the latest technology and again as happened with computing the pace of change was fast. In the late 90's it was deemed a little extravagant to carry a mobile phone almost as a status symbol, the price of calls barring most from participating, and then all of a sudden it became a must have gadget and less of a status symbol. It is much harder now to find someone without a mobile phone than with, all this in little more than 10 years.

Chapter 6

Photography

It is said that currently over 200 thousand pictures are taken every minute around the world. That figure is rising all the time thanks to the continued expansion of mobile phones and tablets. Just think about that for a second, 200 thousand pictures, A SECOND! What on Earth are we taking pictures of? The answer is quite simply everything; pictures of children, holidays and weddings to last night's tea and the odd in-growing toenail. It really is as bizarre as that, in fact even more so, I've been more than polite on what is out there in the ether of the internet.

I'm not here to bore you with a detailed history of photography from its early invention in the late 1800's; you can look that up for yourselves. But the basic points are that some guy with a double-barrelled name discovered how to retain an image on a piece of glass, the process moved on to film, Kodak produced a cheap disposable camera that everyone could afford, colour film was created, photography became mainstream, digital photography was invented and then we're about there. See, not that boring.

As I said at the beginning of the book my story starts around the early 70's, a time when photography was becoming very popular with the masses. There were a number of film styles available, each having a different USP.

There was the cartridge type of camera, easy to load and average pictures. The major disadvantage of the cartridge camera was the limited size of the negative. If you don't know what a negative is, look it up! The 110 cartridge film for example had a negative much smaller than a postage stamp resulting in poor quality pictures and printing any bigger than a postcard size would be far from advisable if you wanted to figure out what the picture was of. Best way is to compare this to an image taken on a digital camera or phone today; the file size would be less than half a megabyte. But these were very popular because of their ease of use and their compact size and that's what mattered. Most of us of a certain age will have some old, strangely coloured and grainy image of our childhood taken on a cartridge based camera; pictures that we would probably prefer didn't exist. 126 cartridge cameras were more or less exactly the same but with a much bigger negative, allowing slightly better pictures but with the downside of the camera being a little bit larger, think three quarters of a megabyte!

There was one other that needs a footnote, the Kodak Disc camera. The film was in a square cartridge that just like the others slotted in to the back of the camera. But the difference was it used a cardboard disc with the negatives fixed uniformly around the outside. No more fiddling around with flimsy strips of plastic, oh no this is all in one. As you would expect there was a downside, quite a big one. You could only take 15 pictures but more than that, the image quality was worse than the 110 cartridge cameras, and that took some beating.

Film technology at the time didn't lend itself well to taking pictures in lower light so we would need a flash to illuminate the subject. But built-in electronic flashguns were a little further in the distance so for now we had to settle for flash cubes. The cube as its name suggests had six sides but only four of them was used. The bottom was used to connect to the camera and the top was blank, well who wants the ceiling to light up? The flash was a silver clad device containing a filament on each face which slotted into a designated hole on the top of the camera and when the shutter was pressed the front facing filament would burst in to life, blinding anyone who dared to be looking at the camera open eyed. That side of the cube was now spent; it had served its purpose. Turn the cube for your next flash and so on. These flash cubes were quite expensive so were not always used resulting in some very dark images with barely recognisable features.

Then in the late seventies the 35mm film came into popular use giving much better quality pictures partly due to its bigger negative and partly due to the continuing development (no pun intended) of the film and camera technology. The film itself was not as easy to load into the camera, being a strip of light sensitive acetate that pulled out of a light sealed canister. There were many manufacturers that created 'easy load' or 'self-loading' cameras to ease the difficulty that this might cause, although this in itself was prone to mishaps due in part to the build quality of the mass produced cameras. Noticeable differences with these cameras were that they included a built in flashgun, no longer did we have the problem of buying expensive cubes, and trying to find them in the house when we needed them, attaching them and being selective on which pictures we used so as not to waste them. No, we just switched the flash on and hey presto, there was light. The 21st century was one step closer.

Of course there was one other type camera that I haven't mentioned; the instant camera. We now call them Polaroid cameras as this was the manufacturer who brought them to life, but there were other companies plying their trade. But much like the vacuum cleaner being referred to as a Hoover or all computer search engines being known as Google (as in, you'll have to Google that), any instant camera became known as a Polaroid. I'm sure there is a technical process in how the picture slowly appeared in front of your eyes, but to a 10-year-old it was pure magic. I recall the concept of wafting the picture in the air or sticking it under an armpit to speed up the process. I'm certain now that it made little difference but it always seemed to work. Two things stand out in my mind, and undoubtedly others too, was the way the picture slid out of the front of the camera like a playing card coming out of a pack. But the noise is one that is unmistakeable, a click, a whirr and a click and out popped your picture. There were as many disadvantages of this format as there were advantages. Actually more disadvantages. Firstly, the film pack only came with 10 pictures meaning you had to be very selective on what you snapped. Secondly there were no negatives, no way to reprint your picture over and over again, and most importantly to a family in the 70's and 80's the film cost a fortune in comparison to normal film, a fact that determined how many pictures you could take, and indeed whether or not you bought the camera in the first place. These cameras were mostly a popular Christmas present for the family and many images I still have are of that period. Polaroid cameras are still around after resurgence in the market from the student area but have generally lost their appeal to film and digital cameras. Imitation is the sincerest form of flattery and many phone apps that allow you to edit images have an option to make your pictures look like old Polaroid pictures. All very retro.

There are very few places you can go where you are not being recorded in some way. CCTV, whether you like it or not owes a lot to this, but there are so many people taking video's on their phones that it is almost impossible to get away from them. A great example of this is the phenomenon that is YouTube. From

76

major disasters to kids running into glass doors, Bungee jumping grannies to cute animals it's all there. It seems that what used to be a special moment captured in time is now so normal and every day that it's hard to get excited about pictures. Ask yourself this question, when was the last time you printed a picture? We don't print pictures now; we save them to the 'cloud'. Can you imagine how that sentence would have sounded 40 years ago? Images are snapped, sent to friends electronically and then stored or deleted. There is now an app that allows you take pictures, send them to your friends and they only last a minute before disappearing forever. Why? I know we now live in a throwaway society but that is taking it one step to far! Every now and then I like to look through my old photos to see how things, mainly me, have changed in the last 20 years or so and I don't have to turn the computer on to do it. Is this really an improvement on how we live our lives? I'm not suggesting for one minute that we should all go back to gathering people around to show off our recent holiday photographs, but the emotional feeling of these images are lost. Ask yourself this question, do you store all your digital images on to a computer and if so when did you last look at any from more than a few months ago? I have digital images of friends and children growing up and it's nice to see them, but it's not the same to go around and show them on a screen, a physical and tangible object gives more of a personal reminiscence. Try it. Look for some old pictures on your computer and 'print' them and next time you visit take them with you. I can guarantee the result will be that much more special than you would ever get holding a screen in front of their face.

I got married a long time before digital photography came along. My photographer used traditional film cameras, he changed films three times giving us a maximum of around 100 pictures to choose from. A couple of weeks later, a selection of pictures was available for us to peruse and choose which ones we would like in our album. Finally, a few more weeks later our wedding album was finished. The process today is quite different. First and foremost, the photographer uses digital cameras. They have, some would argue, a better quality image than film and obviously have no processing time. If needed the couple can see the images long before they are taken away for editing and printing and they can take as many images as they like, subject to the size of their memory card. The pictures are then loaded on to a CD and a photo album is produced in the same way as before except of course the CD.

The 35mm film led to the popularity of the SLR camera (Single Lens Reflex if you must know). All of a sudden everyone could become the next David Bailey (look it up). They were still manual devices that required a certain amount of knowhow to operate them to their best ability, but they definitely kick started the modern day revolution. If I may be so bold as to push the date of this book forward only a couple of years after I left school, which as it's my book I think I can, I recall my first ever SLR camera, an Olympus OM-10. I suppose unless you were into photography at that time this model may mean nothing to you as would many of the other popular cameras at the time like the Pentax ME-Super, Canon AE-1 or the Minolta X300, but this is the one that I broke my teeth on. It wasn't new, I couldn't afford a new one, but it was in full working order and came with everything I needed to take my first ever photograph, but what of? You would think it would be easy to choose, the family or pets or cars for example but I wanted to raise the game, be artistic, more of a David Bailey, so I chose the local park. I got up very early one Sunday morning in winter before the sun rose and biked down to the park looking for 'the' shot. The lake was frozen over, not enough to stand on but enough for the ice to crack in places where the ducks have tried hard to get back in. And then there it was, the picture I had in my mind's eye, a leafless tree, its bare branches hanging over the icy water casting a dull and fuzzy reflection and the Sun just starting to rise behind. I framed the shot, focussed the lens, pressed the shutter and the camera gave a pleasing click reassuring me that the picture will be framed and mounted on the wall for all visitors to see and remark upon. Best take another one just in case the first doesn't work quite right, and as the camera had all these new settings and overrides I thought it would be wise to try out a few different exposures. The film had a maximum of 36 pictures and due to my trigger happy finger and a wish to capture that 'moment' by the end of the morning I only had a few left. Eventually weeks later after I had finished the film, sent it to be developed and printed I collected my masterpieces from the store and prepared to be wowed by my skill. Do you ever get that sinking and disappointing feeling when what you hope for and what you get are miles apart? That was me. Don't get me wrong, the picture was good, in fact it was very good if I say so myself but it wasn't what I had in my mind's eye. But that's how things are.

It's interesting to think that now when I take a photograph I use my mobile phone, I don't bother too much about framing the shot as I can either edit on the computer or more than likely keep it for a while on the phone and then delete it later on. There's no real special feeling to the process, you take a picture or two, show it to friends or post it on one of those social media sites for all and sundry to see and then forget about it. So remember, the next time you take a picture, and I mean of something special, consider the idea of doing more with it then posting it online. Here's a crazy wild idea, why not print it, frame it and hang it, how retro would that be?

Chapter 7

Cinema

Imagine, if you can, a time before multi-screen cinema complexes when a visit to see the latest film involved a trip on the bus to the town centre to a cinema with no more than three screens. The cinemas were not too dissimilar to today's multi-screen complexes, albeit generally in old buildings with dim lights and a well-trodden, dirty and usually for some reason red carpet. Entrance foyers were dark and smelt of a mixture of smoke and popcorn with the odd whiff of body odour from people who had yet to discover the advantage of a regular shower or bath. The remains of old chewing gum and spilt popcorn stuck to your trainers and grumpy dads mumble to each other with the look of resignation knowing that they could be at home with a beer and the TV. Although there were no multi-screen cinemas there were lots of smaller cinemas around the town giving plenty of choice on where to go. These old buildings have now either been knocked down and replaced by new office or retail units or transformed into bingo halls which is a shame.

The screens themselves were of a similar size to todays, and before each screening a curtain would part just as it does today. Trailers and adverts were just as annoying as they are today and would take up yet more time before the main attraction. However, the notable difference was how the movie was projected on to the screen. It was *actually* projected from a projector located in a high position at the back of the room. As the lights went out and the room darkened, the light from the back of the room could be seen like a torch shining up into the night sky. Also, what seemed to be mandatory in those days, smoking was allowed in the cinema too. In fact, there were few places, except maybe in a petrol station forecourt, which you couldn't light up. So as the screen started to flicker into life and the music boomed out of the speakers, the thick blue haze was as visible as mist in the headlights of a car. Again as this was the norm in most aspects of everyday life it wasn't really noticed by many people although I personally found it the worst part of going to the flicks.

As the films were recorded on to large reels, depending on the length of the film, the reel had to be changed half way through. During this interlude the curtains would draw, the lights would glimmer into life and the cinema goers would clamber out of their not particularly comfy seats to do what needed to be done. A highlight of this break for us children was the appearance of the ice-cream lady. Much like you see in theatres now, a lady would stagger across the front of the auditorium carrying an unwieldy tray full of as many e numbers that could be fitted into a tight space. We would advance on to this helpless member of staff in a bid to help her off load some of the heavy burden she was carrying. We toddled back to our seats, pulling down the sprung loaded seat that returned to its upright position and sat there with our legs swinging and tucking into the tub of ice cream. Unfortunately for many children and of course a large number of adults, with the introduction of digital projection this additional excitement of visiting the local picture house has long since disappeared. Eventually, as the visual extravaganza of the film finished and the credits started to roll it was time for the mass exodus from the theatre. By the time you had reached the main exit you would be 2 inches taller after standing in all the dropped popcorn and confectionary. A feature that hasn't changed that much today!

Some of the big releases during my early youth are now considered classics; Jaws, E.T., Star Wars and Star Trek to name but a few. It may be my vague memory fooling me but I feel that the films were in the cinemas for much longer than they are now, no doubt the film studios needed to squeeze as much money from the films as they can before the films had run their course. As I mentioned earlier videos were becoming more popular and film releases eventually made it down to the humble video tape which was good and bad for the studios. On the plus side they would still get some revenue from retail sales but on the negative side the video cassettes would be copied and banded about in a black market playground in a similar way to the computer cassettes I mentioned earlier.

Zoom forward to the present day and things couldn't be much more different. The picture quality in the cinema is far superior, the screens are that bit bigger and the sound follows the action everywhere around the room, and I'm sure it's louder. The films are now available in 3D if you choose to wear those funny glasses, the seats are bigger and comfier with more space between each one and there is smoke free air that no longer hinders the viewing (or breathing) experience, the price of popcorn has however continued to increase. The movies are projected from a digital source negating the need for ice-cream breaks, so not every aspect of the future is better. Films are now released on to DVD's, again an opportunity to be copied although that has been made harder. But there is very little need to copy films as they are released on video streaming channels sometimes only weeks after they have finished at the cinema. So next time you go to the pictures spare a thought about the old lady who used to sell ice cream at the front of the theatre who has been replaced by a large counter full of popcorn sold by the bucket and think about how much half way through the film you'd like an ice-cream but don't want to miss any of the action. There's no half time anymore.

One of the first films I recall going to see was Herbie Goes to Monte Carlo. I went with my parents and siblings to one of the old fashioned cinemas I mentioned earlier but this time in car not bus. Herbie was a Volkswagen Beetle, the old style not the new one. It was white with a stripe going down the centre of the car from the bonnet, over the top and down to the rear bumper and on the bonnet breaking the stripe was the number 53. It was a 'magic' car that had a life of its own that could drive itself, open its doors bonnet and boot at will, sound its horn and flash headlights as a form of communication. As you might expect Herbie was one of the good guys and used its guile to help defeat criminals and foil any illicit plans they may have. As a kid who played with toy cars and gave them their own characteristics it was exactly what I would expect a car to be able to do. My small adventures on the living room carpet were played out on the big silver screen. I'm not suggesting you rush out and buy the DVD or hunt for it on the Sky box, it was one of those films of its era but my nephew watched it when he was around four and thought it was great, which was fantastic as that was one birthday present sorted.

The first film I went to see on my own, or rather without parents but with friends was the James Bond film Moonraker. The film had NASA Space Shuttles flying around space, a space station, hundreds of astronauts with backpacks firing lasers at each other and of course a few obligatory fast chases, this time in speed boats. This was in 1979 around the time that Star Wars and other sci-fi shows were coming out so it was obviously the perfect film for a few pre teenage boys to go and see. It had guns, lasers, spaceships, evil henchmen, gadgets and we had popcorn and fizzy drinks, a perfect match. Many of today's films are sequels or spin offs of original films released in the 70's and 80's. Star Wars and Star Trek made their debut back then and many of the old films have had a makeover for the modern market with lavish new special effects hoping to cash in on the original release. As I write this book Ghostbusters has just been released, Willy Wonka's Chocolate Factory, Superman and even Karate Kid to name but a few although most of these are not a patch on the originals, in my opinion anyway. I think if there's one thing that should be brought back it's the half time interval. It would eliminate the need for people to push by you during the film in order to visit the boys/girls room. It would help avoid the people sat next to you or above you noisily munching their popcorn or hotdog as they would only need to eat during the break, in fact why not make it a rule not to be able to eat whilst the film is showing. The kids would not get quite as fidgety as they wouldn't have to wait as long before they went home. Do you know, I might just send that idea to Odeon/CineWorld/Vue and see what response I get. I think we all know but it's a nice idea.

Chapter 8

Transport

Getting from A to B and back again was just as important then as it is now, probably more so as thanks to modern technology more and more of us are able to work from home, not something easily done in the 70's, and more of the work was manual labour than it is today. Not everyone had a car, let alone two as we do now, consequently the traffic was much lighter on the roads even during 'rush hour'. I'm not saying the roads weren't busy, they were just considerably less busy than today.

Public transport was the main way majority of us travelled to work, school and holidays. The buses that took you to your destination were practical although they lacked today's colourful seating and ergonomically designed curves. As you stepped on to the bus the driver took your money as they do today but where I grew up, and I'm sure it was similar elsewhere, instead of handed him your shrapnel you would drop the coins into a device which looked a little like a car parking meter. You would hear the coins clatter down and then you'd be presented with a small square notched paper in return for your pennies. I've never known if this actually counted the money as once or twice I threw coins in knowing I was a few pence short. To my relief it was never noticed, although I now have a slight guilt in robbing the company of well needed funds, but only slight. However, the more noticeable difference was on the top deck. The seating and décor was the as drab and colourless as downstairs, the spiralling staircase leading upstairs was as much an issue climbing as they are today, and led to a view of the streets as they flew by. But to sit upstairs was an adventure. Obviously it was important, nay vital to get the front seats, which unfortunately were quite often occupied by other such wide eyed children. No matter, a seat upstairs was still a seat upstairs and somehow made you feel older and more grown up. There was a downside to this adventure; we were in the days in which smoking was deemed acceptable in many areas of public life. This particular acceptance lent itself to bus travel but, to make it fair to all passengers; smoking was only permitted on the upper deck. As a child it was unfair, not only would the front seats be taken up with other kids who got on the stop or two earlier or old men puffing away on their woodbines, but also the rear seats were occupied by young adolescents who found it their secret area for covert nicotine intake, increasing the blue mist that engulfed the deck limiting the amount of visibility to 6 feet in front of your face! The lingering smell on their clothes due to the requirement of smokers to sit upstairs would be an ideal excuse to any suspicious parent.

Eventually the journey would come to an end giving one last entertaining feature; ringing the bell. I wouldn't have been able to reach the push button in the old buses as it was not really a button, more of a long strip of rubber running down the centre of the ceiling, replaced today by brightly coloured red buttons attached to every other pole with the tempting word PRESS on it. I did at times step on to the seat beside me and push the bell which usually got a glare from other travellers, but hey, I got to ring the bell and stop the bus so who cares?

Cars were not quite as comfortable then as they are now, electric windows, air conditioning, parking sensors or high quality music systems were the things of the future. We had an old Ford Cortina which was a decent size car with ample space to take me, my 2 brothers and of course Mum and Dad, well someone had to drive. It had faux leather seats or plastic as I'd like to call them which were hot and sweaty in the summer, cold and slippery in the winter, and bear in mind we we're small people at that time so our feet didn't touch the floor, when the car took a corner a little too fast we went sliding across from one side to another like marbles on an ice rink. These cars were built for practicality, not necessarily comfort. There was nothing but each other to stop us, and although seatbelts were fitted to cars back then it wasn't illegal to not wear them, so we didn't. I wouldn't dream of not wearing one now, or even starting the car before everyone is buckled up. Health and safety as we know it was in its infancy, the only general safety advice was given by a large man in a futuristic green suit or a selection of stuffed animals guiding us through the perils of crossing the road. Reading that back that sentence doesn't scan too well unless you knew about the Green Cross Code man and the loveable, sensible Tufty. Cars did have some features you still get in modern vehicles, for example the cigarette lighter. And that's exactly what it was, a device that heated up a removable metal bar that could then be used to light up the nicotine stick, which dutifully turned the inside of the car with the same blue mist you had in the cinema but more concentrated. Today that plug is not called a cigarette lighter it's called a power socket designed to power and charge your mobile phones and Sat-Navs. Which brings on another question, if we were travelling to point B from point A, how did we know where point B was? We relied upon the trusty road atlas, a handily newspaper broadsheet sized booklet normally stuffed in the boot, that would show us exactly where B was. But this road map didn't speak to us or show an imaginary car travelling down a scrolling line or tells us in a patronising voice when we'd gone wrong. The atlas would be generally stored in the boot; I presume on the off chance that we would get in the car drive to a new destination on a whim. And if we did venture to new lands outside of our local neighbourhood these trusty books would come in to their own, although they were probably well out of date by then, new roads having appeared and old ones removed. Regularly the place we wanted to visit lie directly on the fold of the page making it even more difficult to read the direction in time to take the correct exit. I would say sat-navs have removed all these problems and that no-one ever gets lost but there are plenty of tales of sat-navs sending people down roads leading to rivers or lakes but these maybe down to the driver relying on the technology and not their common sense.

It may sound strange to some people but children were allowed to 'walk' to school, on their own without any parental supervision. Ok, obviously I'm not talking about really young children, we weren't that silly but from the age of around 8 or 9 we were sent off with our satchel over our shoulders, walked what was for ten year olds a good distance with the expectation that we would return safe and well after school. Winter time was no different even though it was darker in the mornings and evenings, we were equipped with reflective armbands and a duffle coat to deflect the cold and hopefully any wayward car. It obviously worked for me. Today, there is a mêlée of traffic outside the school gates as parents drop off their precious little bundles even though it's five minutes' walk from home. There is probably more danger of them getting run over at the school gates than walking to school.

Just like today as I got older my 'big school' was further away and I looked to my trusty bike to transport me to my educational establishment. As I mentioned earlier about the cars, safety was also sometimes an afterthought when it came to cycling. Helmets were for motorcyclists or Evel Knievel, not for kids on bikes.

Most bikes didn't have chain guards to stop trouser bottoms catching in them which was a real problem in the 70's as flares were the fashion. Many a good pair of jeans or school trousers were ripped at the bottom thanks in part due to the want to keep fashionable while looking cool on your bike. This is the era when classic bikes were made, Raleigh being the main manufacturer of all the cult bikes. The Chopper, a bike that even now most people have heard of or at least seen, was a strange but cool looking bike; a long seat with backrest (with a warning strip advising that the seat is for one, like that was ever going to happen), a front wheel much smaller than the back, long raised handlebars angles slightly forward just to make it more difficult to steer and finally a gear stick placed right in the middle of cross bar, perfect position for when you slip of the shiny plastic seat. But forget all those slight niggles, it looked cool and was probably one of the easiest bikes to pull a wheelie. If you weren't keen on catching your crown jewels every time you braked the alternative bike was the Grifter. The Grifter was an altogether different beast; a tough no nonsense bike capable of riding on all terrain due to its tractor like tyres, heavily built to take all sort of knocks (a bit like a Tonka toy), gears built in to the hand grips and just for safety a foam covering on the bar that rested between the bars. This was a man's bike. I had one. It was heavy and not easy to pull wheelies on but you could mount curbs without any fear of falling off and you could change gear without taking your hands off the handlebar. It still had street cred but maybe not as much as the Chopper. Younger kids had their own versions of these bikes, the Budgie the shrunken version of the Chopper and the Boxer being the reduced fat version of the Grifter. There are others in this range, some of them being hybrid cross species of the two but the Chopper and Grifter reigned supreme.

No matter what bike you had at some point you had to personalise it. A popular way, and for some reason more popular

89

with girls but by no means exclusive was to attach bread bag tags to the brake cables. I don't think they do bread tags anymore as all the loaves I've seen are tied with plastic strips with the expiry date on them, but back then they were held together with plastic clips of varied colours. I recall some bikes having hundreds on them; heaven knows how much bread their family got through! Stickers were also a popular choice of decoration; footballers, superhero's and cartoon characters being the generic choice but some comics and even some chewing gum and bubble gum packets had stickers to liven up any animate or inanimate object. One thing that was almost compulsory to do when you had a bike was to put an ice lolly stick in between the spokes to create a rat-a-tat-tat noise which although slowed the biked down a bit in our minds sounded exactly like a Harley Davidson.

Then it was time for a change, to become more sensible and grown up. It was time to get a racing bike. You all know what a racing bike looks like, larger wheels and slim tyres, ram horn shaped handle bars, a sharp and un-comfy seat and two gear levers on the front bottom cross bar just in reach of your hands. These machines were built for speed not comfort so how on earth the Tour-de-France cyclists manage to go up hills on them is a mystery to me. Come rain or shine these trusty steeds would guide you through the thickest of traffic, which as I mentioned earlier wasn't as bad as today, at a reasonable pace to school but a lot quicker on the way home! As winter and the dark nights drew in it was important that you made yourself visible to other road/pavement users. Bike lights during that period were not as small or as bright as today's LED versions; the 70s and 80s lights were big bulky devices made of plastic, usually cream coloured and used large D sized batteries. They had a big circular glass front behind which was a silver reflector and in the centre the bulb, a normal incandescent bulb not LED. Stand one next to today's bike lights and there is no comparison on brightness, it would be like comparing a couple of candles to a house light but back then is was bright. They attached to the bikes via a metal bar which fitted under the handle bars or on the front wheel arm. They weren't great, they didn't flash, they weren't bright and the batteries didn't last very long, but they were what we had and they did the job. I recall having a dynamo light set which consisted of a small flywheel which could be pressed against the wheel when needed, cables running to the front and back lights. As you might know a dynamo generates power by turning the wheel and so the bike lights would come to life while I was moving, but not when stopped. Also the faster I went the brighter the lights appeared which as good an incentive as I needed to go fast.

So there we are; cars that had as much safety regulations as papier-mâché fire guard, bikes that were fashionable and positively dangerous and not necessarily practical to ride, lights that gave just about adequate illumination for others to see you, flared trousers that would snag and cause you to fall and no helmets to save you from any imminent danger. It's amazing that any of us survived long enough to tell the tales.

Chapter 9

Seasons

I know everyone's childhood when looking back is the best time to be young, and I feel the same. But remember, this book is about the era I grew up in and as such I can confidently and justifiably say the seventies and eighties were the best time to grow up. I feel justified when I say to the children of today 'you've got it easy, we never had that when I was your age'. When talking about the past we always relate to physical, tangible objects that have changed, been replaced or just disappeared into the ether of history. But there are other pastimes and subjects that you can't touch but are nonetheless etched into my memory. 'Is Carl coming out to play', or 'we're going to park, coming for a game of football'? are phrases that linger in my mind reminding me of the days when I was able to play a full day's worth of football without needing food or a break, and then nipping home for tea before going out for a ride on the bike. Seasons were also in their correct order and obeyed the rules of nature, Sun in summer, falling leaves in autumn, snow and dark nights in winter and new flowers and greenery appearing in the spring. These rules were set in stone by the images made on classroom walls by children encouraged by traditional teachings past down from generation to generation.

Summer holidays, or six weeks holiday as it was often known, were a time of endless sunshine requiring tubs of sun cream being liberally slapped on the shirtless backs of the footballer wannabe's. Gallons upon gallons, or litres if you prefer of water were continually sprayed on garden lawns, cars were regularly washed and paddling pools were filled with tiny tots. Trees were not only full of essential light gathering leaves but of kids hanging from branches trying to make it from one tree to another without the breakage of any major bone. The pavements, once the area for pedestrian use was now a race track for the bikes that were bought for Christmas but had seen little use since the festive season due to inclement weather. The shouts and shrieks of children playing in the streets were regularly interrupted by the jingling tunes of the ice cream van. Rockets, Twisters, ninety nines, Screwballs and Magnums to name but a few were consumed in as much quantity as mums' purse would allow, fizzy drinks with enough trapped pressure to launch a rocket into space and sweets containing more e-numbers than the length of Pi were the daily diet of any self-respecting child. Street warfare took place on the school field by means of the obligatory game of football. There were no rules, no offsides, no yellow cards and definitely no limit on how many players each team had. Most sensible schools dismantled their goalposts long before the holidays started so the posts were piles of coats and jackets leading to the phrase 'jumpers for goalposts'. All too soon the end of the holidays loomed in to view, homework was rushed through to get finished just in time for the first day of school and the hey-days of fun seemed a distant memory.

Autumn appeared from no-where. One minute the sun was high and strong in the blue and white cloud covered sky, and then it was lower down casting long shadows. Trees started to lose their leaves, those still hanging on turned to beautiful shades of orange and gold before letting go and joining the wet mounds gathering on the streets. As the nights started drawing in, the once busy streets became quieter, bikes started to go the same way of the small animals and got put into hibernate for the rest of the year. Horse chestnut trees changed their names for the season and became the giver of the knuckle breaking conker. The game was on to find the strongest conker, and what alchemy could be used to prolong its life; soaking in vinegar and roasting in the oven I recall being a popular yet ineffective choice, but not with the parents. We looked forward to darker nights when the bonfires would be lit, households locked away their pets for safety and the sales of potatoes increased tenfold. Children with hats, gloves and scarves lovingly knitted by Grandma would be carefully chaperoned to a safe position looking at the communal bonfire whilst madly waving a sparkler through the air. Flocks and flocks of birds would fly south to warmer climes, the evening sky filling with the dark shapes like a flight of aeroplanes setting off to war.

And then it was winter. Even back then there seemed to be no definitive time that winter started, it just happened. The nights got colder, the streets were devoid of children and the air was filled with the smoke from coal fires. The orange glow of the street lights showed the icy rain being fiercely blown at right angles and the silhouettes of workers rushing home with hunched shoulders with the hope that this would somehow protect them from the storm brewing around them. It snowed, it always snowed in winter. Snowball fights and the building of snowmen were a staple diet of winter days in the seventies. Milk bottles that were delivered in the early hours of the morning would have their foil tops pecked open by the birds searching for the cream. The town centres became flooded with Christmas lights and the streets crowded as parents, husbands and wives desperately threw their money into the ringing tills in a bid to get the latest must have presents carefully selected from the plentiful Christmas catalogues strewn around the house. Christmas Day, and the roads filled with cars travelling to relatives who no more wanted their visitors than the visitors wanted to go, but it was Christmas and that's what you do. The New Year arrived with the traditional pomp and ceremony of parties, fireworks and the gongs of Big Ben marking the start of the end of winter.

Winter faded into spring and as the days started getting longer, the Sun struggled through the clouds bringing life to dormant plants. Daffodils, snowdrops and bluebells appeared overnight showering the flowerbeds and grass verges with colours that had been absent for months. The birds, those who'd stayed behind, silent during the dark months found their voices and used them as early as they could almost in fear that they may lose them again. The flocks started to fill the skies once again returning to their homes. Chocolate eggs covered the shelves and children's faces as Easter loomed in to view and parents spent their evenings working on cardboard and paper bonnets for the obligatory school parade. But the weather in all these seasons remained true to their remit, hot in summer, cold in winter, dull and dark in autumn and cool but colourful in spring. Today, summer is no longer one long period of blistering heat and winter has very little snow to talk about. I don't see kids climbing trees and even the good old game of conkers has fallen foul of the health and safety brigade.

Life seemed so innocent back then, bikes, football, ice-cream and continuous sunshine were the norm. Families across the land gained extra kids to feed during the holidays as we moved from one friend's house to another to play games and be duly fed along with the rest of the family. The odd phone call from parent to parent informing them of the whereabouts of their offspring would satisfy any worries that may be apparent after a certain amount of time. Our skin would peel off after being in the ever present sun too long without any adequate protection, later being cured by the liberal application of calamine lotion. We would walk a mile on our own to see our friends or go to the park only to find them not there and then saunter home without any questions asked from anyone. In winter we would make large snowmen out of the ever falling snow storms, our fingers and toes numb with the cold which stung as we went home and put them in front of the fire. Christmas was magical as slowly each house erected their Christmas tree and proudly displayed it in front of the window to announce that Christmas had arrived in their household. Concertina style paper folded hanging decorations clung to the ceilings and tinsel adorned every visible surface leaving just enough space for the deluge of Christmas cards from family and friends. The house would smell of roast turkey and the television would be on a continuous stream of adverts for the wide eyed expectant kids. I look back now with my own rose tinted glasses and realise that the era I grew up in was probably the best time to be a kid.

Chapter 10

Education

I wouldn't have thought schools would have changed that much in the last forty years or so but I'd be wrong. Yes of course children still have lessons in a classroom with a teacher droning on about Pythagoras's theorem or nouns, pro-nouns and verbs, but the classroom itself has changed dramatically. My primary school of which I have fond memories, if not a little vague in places, was a smallish single storey building with around 6 or 7 classrooms, a large playing field and a decent sized playground.

Its main hall had parquet flooring which was polished and buffed to an inch of its life, ideal for sliding on and had a wonderful smell of something new as if it had just been newly laid for the first time. Each morning we would sit on this floor, crossed legged and listening intently, well as intently as 5 and 6 year olds could, to the head teacher praising children on their behaviour or school work over the last week. Those who did exceptionally well would receive a merit badge which would be worn with pride for the rest of the week, of course I had the pleasure of wearing it on many occasion, honest. Although looking back I'm not sure it was awarded for anything, I think they were just handed out on regular basis so each child had a turn of being good that week which sort of takes the shine off it a bit. At the end of assembly we would sing the Lord's Prayer and then file silently out in our class groups to our classrooms. Lessons would be interrupted in the morning with the arrival of the milk. In the 70's milk was given to every school child under the age of 7 by the government, which later in the decade a certain Mrs Thatcher, who later became the Prime Minister, removed this process giving her the nickname of 'the milk snatcher'. I'm pretty sure that if we offered today's school kids a bottle of warm milk with a layer of thick cream on the top and a straw to poke through the metal foil lid there wouldn't be many takers. Each week a different pupil would be selected to be the milk monitor that at the time sounded a very grown up title, one that came with important responsibilities, primarily being the one who that collected the beverages and then returned the empty bottles. At the end of the day our teacher would sit us round and read us stories, again I'm sure this happens today. Finally, before the bell rang we would put our chairs on the desk, grab our satchels and prepare for the dash home.

Many of the lessons, as you would expect from a primary school were educational disguised as fun. Rudimentary counting and times tables were taught in chants, 'two twos' are four, three twos' are six' and so on and the alphabet had a tuneful ring to it. Think

98

about it; try to say the alphabet without breaking into the tune you learned at school. There were plenty of arts and crafts sessions, I recall creating a picture of a Kingfisher made from coloured foil and feathers stuck to card by PVA glue and spots of paint from a plastic palette tray with round indentations to mix the colours. It was of course in my eyes a true reflection of what a Kingfisher looked like and so realistic you'd expect it to fly off the paper at any time. I'm sure in essence it looked like a few bits of feathers stuck to some card but then if you look at Picasso's pictures they're hardly realistic are they and they fetch a fortune! On the desk would be a jam jar filled with water for cleaning the brushes which would be black due to the large amount of mixed colours from all the brushes the other kids have dipped in. The most important part of any classroom was PVA glue. It was dispensed via a conical shaped semi translucent container with an angled head that released the glue when pressed against the papers and if you got your hands covered in it, as you obviously would, it peeled off like an unwanted layer of skin. We would inflate balloons, cover them in papier-mâché and pop the balloons giving us scope to create a disembodied head, gruesome stuff for a 6-year-old. The desks would be littered with half used and broken wax crayons (made by Crayola), the preferred tool for colouring in, and coloured pencils which would be used for the finer details, their ends chewed and nibs bent or broken. Other kids would be happily cutting up bits of Play-Doh with rounded safety scissors then mixing all the colours together to render another box useless. Is it just me or did Play-Doh have a sweet, slightly sickly smell? I haven't had the need or reason to get my hands on any of it for a very long time (about 40 years) and I've always wondered if that smell is still there. I'll put that on my bucket list of things to do.

In the summer we would have our school sports day on the playing field, an area that was normally out of bounds until the heat waves that I've mentioned we received every year. Bean bags, skipping ropes and hoola-hoops were brought out of storage and used for the usual variety of sporting activities that prepared any child for the next Olympics should there be a coloured bean bag throwing competition added to the events. The sack race was one of the highlights of the day for me. Large hessian sacks would be dragged out from some old musty cupboard; a child placed within and made to hop down a marked out track on the field. Now you may call me an old romantic but I think this is the sort of fun that is missing in today's health and safety brigade world. Parents who had limbered up the whole summer for the compulsory race eyed up the competition marking out the ones to watch whilst stating it was just a bit of fun.

During the periods we were not allowed on the grass fun was had on the playground. Footballs at our school were banned mainly because the school was adjacent to a busy road and the off chance that a wild shot might make it over the fence was enough to remove them from the playground activity. So, in the absence of said spherical object we fashioned our very own alternative from socks. Sock-ball as it was known had all the same rules of under 8's playground footy, namely a free-for-all but the replacement ball was made of lots and lots of socks tightly bound together. Admittedly it slowed the game down a bit, the ball didn't bounce and the option for dribbling was severely restricted but the game carried on none the less. If football wasn't your thing other less active games could be had. Marbles would be played around the edges of the playground and those marbles that were won were carried in old socks that managed to evade capture from the football frenzied kids. At the end of playtime a teacher would stand at the front of the school doors and blow a whistle at which point every child stopped what they were doing and froze still. Then after a few seconds, when the teacher was happy that everyone had obeyed the command the whistle was blown again and everyone lined up in the classes ready to file in to the school. Little did I know that school was not going to be this much fun for ever; the junior school was creeping up on me.

From being a moderate sized fish in a smallish pool where all the teachers knew your name to being a very small fish in a vast ocean was a massive shock to the system. All of a sudden things started to get serious, even the compulsory school uniform conditioned pupils into the regimented way of life that would dominate their education until the very end. Of course rebellions took place and the uniforms were quite often worn in a more personalised way. Top shirt buttons would be undone and ties would be worn with as large a knot that could possibly be tied, the thin end being tucked into the shirts that were quite often hanging out. The sweet smell of newly polished parquet flooring was a thing of the past to be replaced by the stale smell of the great unwashed. The corridors echoed with the sound of aforementioned rebellious kids who were not intending to get a great deal from their education years, who no doubt probably went on to be a professor of science or something. But things weren't all bad, old friends came with us to the new school and new friendships were forged over the first few months as slowly and steadily we started to become comfortable with our new surroundings.

So how are things different to today's educational environments (schools to you)? Well consider the teachers main aid, the board where all the relevant information is displayed on; the blackboard. Large blackboards would be fixed to a wall at the front of the classroom, a quantity of half broken sticks of chalk in varying colours resting on the ledge at the bottom of the board along with the blackboard rubber.

The blackboard rubber was an amazing device, not only was it used to remove information and rude words written by rebellious pupils but it was used as an effective long distance weapon. Teachers would accurately hurl them across the room while shouting the pupils name, not normally hitting the child but giving a near enough miss to bring them in to line, a policy which I'm sure would be frowned upon today, and rightly so. There were also hi-tech blackboards, well sort of hi-tech, they were on a roller and effectively doubled the size of writing area. I don't think, and I'm happy to be corrected on this, that any modern day schools use blackboards, now preferring to use the interactive white boards. It's true these new-fangled screens are a much better teaching aid and remove the chance of inappropriate words and symbols appearing on the screen, but it's not the same as getting covered in chalk dust and going home with a bruise and having to explain the error of your ways to your parents.

Back then we used exercise books to write all our homework and class work in. Emblazoned on the front cover was the school crest and lines for you to write your name and class number neatly on the top. Although the books were brightly coloured for some reason it was recommended that the books should be covered or 'backed'. All manner of paper could be used to cover the front and back pages, some opting for thick wrapping paper or art and craft style paper, but for many it was down to wallpaper left over from the last room decoration in the house. This was one of the first times some of us would be introduced to class snobbery. The 'posh' kids would have lovely floral embossed paper whilst others would have simple stripes or even woodchip paper. Sometimes the teacher would mark the homework during the lesson while we got on with work he'd set. The books would be piled on the side of his desk and as each book was covered differently it was sometimes possible to spot your own book amongst the pile. Hope was high that your book would be lower in the deck as you know your homework was not up to scratch and the bell would go before your book reached the top. It never happened for me, he must have sorted the books into an order of quality wrapping putting the cheap ones on the top. I'm led to believe this practice is still in place in many schools but for the purpose of this book I'd like to claim that this process was invented and perfected during my school days, although I stop short of actually claiming the whole idea of my own. Pencils and crayons were no longer the tools for writing replaced by the grown up fountain pen. Fountain pens were a totally new experience, writing with what was in all intents and purposes a quill minus the feather. They were, or at least could be messy; leaving the pen on the paper too long or tapping it with your finger and ink would flow and blot the paper. Little plastic ink cartridges essential for the productivity of the work would quite often split in your pencil case and consequently in your school bag or strategically left on the floor ready to be stood on with the obvious hilarious outcome, or was that just my school?

Break time, no longer called playtime, that's too childish, had less running around and more gathering together like prisoners in a prison of war camp. The corridors of the school were out of bounds during this leisure time patrolled by the school prefects. Prefects were children who were selected for their sensibility, although there were always a number of non-sensible pupils who slipped through the net. Privileges were bestowed upon these chosen few, the primary one was to be allowed to wander the corridors during lunch time while the peasants were kept outside in all weathers. Indeed, the major role of the prefects was to keep these lowly deprived nobodies out of the school during the breaks and to monitor any disruption that may occur. Nothing did really occur and the benefit of patrolling the school was limited to the dark and wet winter days while during the blistering summer we would watch as the kids that were on the better side of the glass door tan themselves during every day heat waves.

This is the era when digital watches started to become more than just a time piece reminding you of how long you had before the last bell rung. The addition of a calculator was full of controversy, should they be allowed in to the classroom? If they were allowed it was strictly prohibited that they should be used during lessons, which sort of defeated the object of having one. But for those who had the advantage of sitting at the back of the class there was always the opportunities to gain advantage of this pocket wonders. That being said to operate them was a challenge in itself. The keys were tiny as you would expect and were best operated by the use of the sharp end of a ballpoint pen lid. Some of these watches also played rudimentary games due to the limited layout of the LCD's but at least it was another distraction from Archimedes principle of getting water from a bath. Today we have mobile phones that will calculate any sum or equation for us as well as tell us what year the fountain pen was invented.

Just as you were getting used to this more grown up environment you were pushed out the door to your next and final stage of schooling. Senior school was the business end of education, where all your hard work would come to fruition and you would walk out of that school a fully grown adult ready to walk in to the arms of desperately waiting employers, although it didn't always pan out that way. Lessons became more serious and were whittled down to the subjects that would suit your future employment, if of course you knew by then what it was you actually wanted to do. Most people, and that included me didn't have a clue what we wanted to do, but not to worry the school provided a career advisor to find out what job you would be suited to. First question; what are your interests and hobbies? Personally I played football, delivered newspapers, played computer games, read comics and rode my bike. His suggestion; become a postman. This scenario played out throughout the school, each child given a generic job suggestion according to what he thought they were capable of doing. If you liked playing with toy trains he would suggest a train driver, if you liked to take pictures obviously you'd be a photographer and if you liked to play Monopoly you'd either work in a bank or become an estate agent. It really was that generic.

Exams were a big part of this school period, and still are. Each term was spent cramming almost parrot fashion information into our little heads, whether we wanted it there or not, to see us through the tedious period of sitting in silence in the main hall with 40 to 50 other pupils desperately trying to hide their digital watches and arms that had some clues to the answers written on them while a teacher would slowly walk around peering over shoulders just to make you more nervous than you were to start with. Weeks would go by until your results would arrive telling you that you have successfully gained enough qualification to become a postman, train driver or an estate agent. Just for the record, I didn't take up the suggestion of being a postman; they don't read comics or play football, what sort of a job is that?

105

Education hasn't changed in the years since I was a child but the way in which it is taught has. Lessons that we had that were separate in their own right have now been amalgamated into bigger groups; cookery and needlework are now home economics, the sciences are the combined name for physics, biology and chemistry and even French or German lessons are now just called the modern foreign languages as if it's too difficult to split them up. Schools are no longer drab dark grey buildings with as much life as a rock but bright colourful and welcoming places that almost make it a pleasure to go to school. Technology has replaced old ways of communication and interaction; subjects can be studied on line rather than old reference books and rather than talk in the playground kids hunch over their mobile phones checking their Facebook pages. Maybe in another forty years we will do away with schools altogether and learn everything online.

Chapter 11

The New World

When I was 5 years old we moved house to a brand new housing estate which in many parts was still being built. The house we moved from was old, very old. It was what used to be called a two up, two down which meant exactly that, two rooms upstairs and two rooms downstairs and very little else. As far as I knew the house had not been modified, since it was built probably around the early 1900's, although obviously basics like electricity and plumbing had been installed, which meant it was bereft of all the other benefits of modern houses. For example, and I know this will be somewhat unbelievable but at the time to a five-year-old it was the norm, we had no indoor bathroom, which in turn leads to the fact we also had no inside toilet. The only heating was from a fire in the living room; of course I mean in a fire place not in the centre of the room, it wasn't that old!

But it was cold in the winter. We didn't have the luxury of double glazed windows ours were sash windows, one window frame on top of the other but over lapping so they could slide over each other. The bottom window would push up in front of the top frame, although if I remember correctly there was a think cord attached to some pulleys on the side, a steady pull would ease them up and down. This single glass pane's along with the wooden frame they were set in, which themselves were far from flush. We had thick blankets, two or three depending on the season, not duvets with all their tog ratings, but we were warm.

In the absence of a bath we had a tin bathtub hung up outside in the back yard which was brought in and placed in front of the fire. Pans and buckets would be filled with hot water from the kitchen; yes, we did actually have hot running water, and tipped into the tub. Obviously my memory of all this is limited as I was only five so I'm sure there are bits I've missed out but I think you get the general gist. One good thing about all this primitive cleaning routine was that as the tub was in the living room in front of the fire we could also watch the TV while getting a bath, now I bet you can't do that. OK maybe if you used a mobile phone or tablet but that's cheating.

When it came to do the business of relieving yourself of excess baggage (going to the loo) there was no other option but to go outside which in the summer time was not that bad even on an evening. However, as winter drew in and it got colder and darker the adventure was not quite the same. Remember I was five, not quite keen on the dark especially in a cold and lonely back yard, the toilet seemingly a long way from the house, the bogey man waiting behind the gate certainly made toilet breaks go by very quickly.

As they demolished the rows of houses we used to call home we moved in to the new house and it was like moving into the light. If you've ever seen The Wizard of Oz which you must do sometime in your life, you'll know the beginning scenes. Dorothy is stuck in a small farm with the basic facilities and this part of the movie is shot in black and white. The house is whisked in to the air by a vicious tornado, household objects are thrown around in the usual dramatic fashion until the house lands squarely on top of the wicked witch. Dorothy opens the door and is hit by an extravaganza of colour and light. Moving to the new house was a little like that, with the obvious exception of the spinning house and witch. We had an indoor toilet; in fact we had two and a bathroom. We had central heating and three bedrooms, a kitchen and dining room and even a garden not a back yard, in essence we had what we all have now and take for granted, but it was to me a truly amazing change in lifestyle.

We weren't a rich family by any stretch of the imagination but we weren't poor compared to some families, we sat somewhere near the middle. We lived in a rented council house which until the early 80's when the government promoted the option of buying your own house, was quite normal. We always had food in the cupboards, plenty of clothes to wear and received presents at Christmas and birthdays, in short we wanted for nothing. And that is what I see as one of the differences to today's children. Yes they have all the above, food, clothes and toys but they still want more, and quite often get it. For some reason parents and grandparents pander to every request from the offspring. 'Can I have the latest game for the Playstation / XBox, it's only £50' or 'I *need* those new trainers, they're only £80'. If it keeps them quiet and in some ways, more importantly keeps them up with the neighbour's kids then they ultimately get it. If I wanted the latest board game or gadget when I was a kid because little Jonny next door but one had it then it wasn't going to happen. It wasn't that my parents were being mean, it wasn't because they didn't love me, it was because it was an expense that they could ill afford to spend, and that was that. Did it make me bitter and twisted? No, it made me understand that you don't always get what you want, and if you wanted to play one these games you needed to make friends with Jonny. We didn't crave branded clothing, three stripes on my shirt sleeve made no difference to how the shirt was worn or indeed how quickly it got dirty. Its exorbitant price offered us the opportunity to get two shirts for the price of the one regardless of the badge on the corner.

As I said the housing estate was still in the throes of being built and as such there were many half-built houses and in places just the footings on show, an ideal adventure playground for a young lad. We climbed staircases long before they were safe, used the footings as trenches for our warfare and rolled down large mounds of mud and clay just because they were there. We used the house shells as our gang huts and made our marks on the fresh wooden beams to mark our territory. Somewhere in one or two, actually probably a lot more than that, if you took the walls back to the plaster boards and revealed the timbers underneath you would find some etched out initials of mine and my friends made way back in the seventies. It will never be quite like finding Tutankhamen's tomb but it would certainly be a small time capsule that I would be very happy to see, although I'm sure the house owner wouldn't be so pleased.

There were smells that even now take me back to that time; freshly cut wood and sawdust, cement drying and even newly dug clay remind me of that time in my life where everything was care free, as long as you weren't caught by the night watchman. All the houses on the estate had small wooden fences comprising essentially of two planks of wood fixed horizontally and parallel to concrete posts. They were no more than two feet tall and each garden had a lawn and garden path, you could see all the way down the street with nothing to get in the way. My house backed on to a road and on the other side was our school; we couldn't have got much closer if we tried. From our back garden we could see straight into the playground and the front entrance of the school, we had no excuse for being late! I have a photograph of me when I was probably around eight or nine walking down the garden path in my grey school jumper, wide collared shirt and flared trousers, and in the background was the playground and school. At some point in time, and I can't really remember when, fences were built around gardens. Big six foot fences blocking the outside world from looking in and consequently blocking the view from inside. Now as I return to the house where my parents still live it doesn't look like the estate I grew up in, there is no community spirit, everyone has confined themselves to their own small holdings and only speak if they need to. They know their nearest neighbours, maybe for a couple of houses either side but nothing more. New tenants move in and leave and no one knew who they were. Front doors are locked, and rightly so, security lights are aimed directly down drives and paths and are activated well past the boundary of the garden. The school is now locked down on a night with large shutters, the type you would see in a High Street store. I know this can be a generalisation and some areas of towns and cities are a lot more open but things have changed and I for one don't think it's all for the better.

So there we are, we have moved from the innocent days of the early 1970's where everything was care free, the sun shone every day and the seasons behaved themselves. Technology was basic but functional, front doors were unlocked and kids would burst through them demanding money for the ice cream man. Health and safety were by words that didn't mean a great deal put together, cuts, bruises and broken bones were the accepted part of growing up, bikes ruled the footpaths, trees were natures climbing frames and school fields were for football. Milk was delivered to your house by the milk man instead of being purchased during your weekly shop and penny sweets actually cost a penny.

The early 1980's were my introduction to modern life when computing and gaming were in their infancy, TV's were getting bigger, and smaller TV's were becoming part of the bedroom furniture. Video's negated the need to visit the cinema and cars became more comfortable and a little safer. Ten years is all it took to get from one stage of my life to another but the world changed dramatically in that time, and it continues to do so. From the 80's to now the world has changed again with 24-hour news, 100's of TV channels, mobile phones and with social media ruling our every waking moment it is easy to see the rapid advancement in technology since then. But this book has been about my journey through early childhood and what changed.

Have I fulfilled my purpose for writing this book? Well that's up to you to decide for yourself. Your history of this time may vary slightly from mine but I'll wager by not much. I wonder what my nephew's book will be like in forty years' time.

As is customary at the end of most books, and who am I to break with customs and traditions, I would like to dedicate this book to those who have helped, those who have endured and those who have suffered during its long and staggering journey to the end. Those who have hindered do not get a mention.

Of course my wife Claire must come first, she more than anyone has had to show immense patience whilst listening to me ramble on about how good things were in the past (which as this book proves they were). Her unwavering support has helped push me on when I felt it was going nowhere, her ideas from her own childhood and the constant cups of tea and biscuits that sustained me and drove me to the end.

I must also thank Lewis my nephew who without his existence the book would never have left my fingers and found its place on a screen. He may be young now but he will eventually get to the stage of life where he may want to record his thoughts of his past, and hopefully this book will inspire him.

To my brother Graham who shared this period of my life and gave me so many happy memories of the technology we learned to use and the games we played. Even though he pressed symbol shift and my player kicked the ball too early in Match Day 2!

Special thanks to Dean Curtis whose tender years belay his knowledge and helped give this book its title, to Jane England whose memory of all things passed have been of great help, to Jimmy Grassby who's enthusiasm has been infectious and thank you to all those who have added input, criticism and ideas to make this book what it is.

And finally thank you to my parents who brought me into this world and gave me the upbringing that nurtured my passion for technology, gave me freedom to be myself and put up with all the tantrums expected and delivered from a young boy.

Printed in Great Britain
by Amazon